to Rohan and Srijita

**Simple methods to
RISE and get RAISE in the organisation**

WORK
WORKS

GIRISH TIWARI

INDIA • SINGAPORE • MALAYSIA

ISBN 979-8-89363-970-4

When one is about to finish college, particularly in the final year, the buzzword is "campus placement." Some colleges conduct special mock sessions on "how to excel in interviews." The internet is flooded with various types of tests like logical reasoning, numerical ability, non-verbal reasoning, and aptitude tests to help you perform well in the tests conducted by organisations in the first round of campus recruitment process. In the past, the breaking news used to be what packages organisations offered in certain management and engineering colleges across the country. The breaking news used to focus on what the top performers in a college were offered as a package. Families are keen to know which company one secured a job with and what the package entails. This indicates that as one nears completion of studies, society and family are curious to learn about the job offer and organisation.

On the flip side, some individuals decide to change jobs, especially within a year or two of completing their studies, due to reasons such as the temporary nature of their current job (contractual), feeling of a misfit in their role, dissatisfaction with the package compared to what their classmates are earning, or social pressure to secure a "good" company job.

This book is for those who have been selected by an organisation and have just started working or are currently searching for a job and will soon start working. It is also for those who have started working but are unhappy with their first or second job and wish to change. Additionally, it's for those who have already changed jobs in their early years of working and for those who want to establish themselves in their job, aiming to grow within the organisation and build their career.

You studied hard and are among the fortunate few who secured a job with an organisation. The organisation where you landed a job might have been of your choice, or you may have had no choice but to join it. Perhaps you received offers from multiple organisations and chose this one, or this was the only offer you received. Let me tell you, it does not matter in the long run because you will likely embark on a 36 to 40-year journey (approximately), depending on your current age. This is what we call a career, which typically lasts around 40 years. We will delve into careers more deeply in the later part of this book. In the first part, I will cover how to make the most of whatever start you get and how each action of yours influences your career journey. Now that you are inside an organisation and settled into a role (post your induction, etc.), the question is: Is it over? Is it done? Or is it just the beginning?

Even if this is not your first job but a second or third one within 2 to 3 years of joining an industry, you can still see it as a "beginning!"

You must utilise the formative years of your career effectively to achieve professional success. Professional success not only brings monetary rewards but also fulfills your aspirations, which are fundamental to any individual's life. Monetary rewards or remuneration remain stagnant if solely based on years of service and annual increments. However, they increase exponentially if you grow professionally and demonstrate your value to organisations.

As I write this book, I believe that securing your first job or a subsequent job early in your career is just a "start." Your qualifications, your rank in college, your understanding of subjects, and your in-depth knowledge are what enable you to enter an organisation. During interviews for your first job, academic questions are asked. From this point onward, although you start earning, your earning growth, career growth, professional development, and personal growth depend significantly on what you do from now on—not just what you've done so far (which was studying). Indirectly, these aspects also shape your personality as a human being.

The world you inhabited until now, while you were studying, was quite different. Most of the time, you were not in direct competition with your classmates on a daily basis. Exams were held at discrete intervals, and assessments were not comparative. There was no limit to how many students could score full marks. Society viewed you as "learners" and thus didn't expect much beyond your studies. Your family, society, and government-provided various supports to facilitate your education.

Let me explain further: generally, until you reach the age of 22, everyone—family, society, friends—expects you to gain knowledge, acquire skills, primarily learn and grow, and do these things very well. There is minimal expectation from you to deliver or contribute significantly during this period; the assumption is that you're preparing and equipping yourself to contribute later.

During studies, it's possible for all students to score full marks in a subject. While competitive exams do have rankings, they typically involve a larger pool of students. However, within an organisation, your comparisons are within smaller groups, possibly even within your own team, where your next-desk colleague becomes your competitor.

In a typical middle-class family, it's assumed that by the age of 22, one should study well and acquire the right education and skills to lead a good life, supporting not only oneself and one's family but also contributing to society.

However, the question is, is this enough, or is qualification only a foundation of sorts which, to begin with, places individuals in a position from where onwards their second journey starts, the journey which relatively is more competitive, much longer, lengthier in terms of time, complex in terms of activities as many more dealings are with human behaviour and hence highly challenging. In this journey, there is no set syllabus, there are many more variables, exams do not get held on a prescribed date, there are no past year exam papers for you to practice, and there is no structured tutoring mechanism. There is a saying that either you sail or you sink.

In the classroom, teachers do have a system of evaluation, but that is much more discreet (based on VIVA, written tests, Practical in laboratories, etc). However, what happens in the organisation and in the marketplace is totally different. Here, the evaluation is a lot granular and highly abstract.

So, one must be much more prepared and attentive in his / her behaviour, actions, etc, so as to excel in the organisation and, hence, career.

You are going to spend nearly 40 years from now on; I have already spent 40 years in the industry, so what I am going to do in this book is share with you what I saw as effective for an individual, what I saw as ineffective or counterproductive for an individual in the long run in an organisational environment. I will also bring in what I have learned based on my observations about some individuals whom I had the opportunity to mentor, especially in the early part of their careers. I will be quoting examples from individuals, events, sports, politics, etc. However, it all will be only from the point of view of extracting learning from it in our own area of "work."

I will be unwinding my 40-year Cassette and will share with you many things; as we proceed, we will make some theories out of it; if you get convinced, you can attempt to practice it and try it out; in case you do not consent with me its fine as well. The theories are very simple, actionable and implementable. Actions are to be taken by an individual (self) in almost all cases. So, as you read this book, you can go into the mode of actions and start trying them.

# Comparison: It is a relative world; things keep evolving here.

Whether we agree or not, this world has a lot of relativity and keeps comparing things to make decisions. Assessment happens regularly, whether we like it or not. It is natural that a player is compared with past players, a leader with his/her predecessors, an employee with colleagues or even someone who previously held the same role or position. You will be surprised to learn that even within families and among family members, this evaluation happens in a relative manner, and comparisons take place. During your college days, didn't you among students used to compare various professors? When one makes these comparisons, various criteria are deployed, which are decided in the mind based on needs or importance.

If we say this is natural, then the question is how this comparison is done and what parameters are used. We will limit ourselves to the organisational perspective. But as we reach the end of this book, you will agree that it can also be applied outside the organisation, such as in society and family.

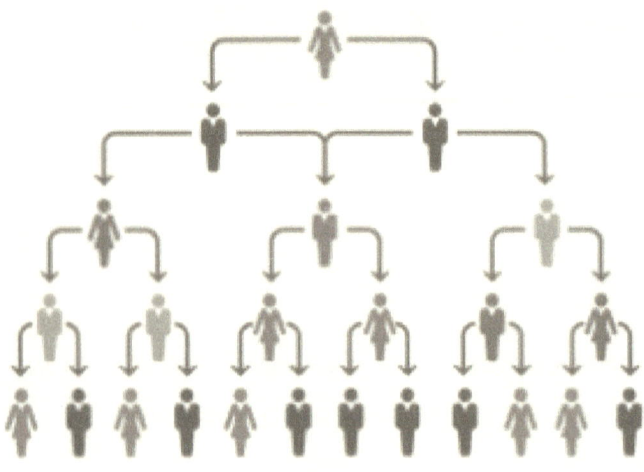

Fig 1

Remember, an organisation is described in the shape of a pyramid (Fig 1). It simply shows that as we go up in the organisation, fewer and fewer people are seen, and positions become less in number. It also means that from the bottom layer, only a few move to the next layer. From the next layer, only a select few progress to the third layer, and so on, until the person at the top stands alone. How is this done? If there is a process, what is the process? How are these people who move up selected by the organisation, and what parameters are deployed in doing this?

When a team or organisation performs well, there is a system of annual rewards where a team leader is required to reward their team members based on their contribution to good work. The organisation may allocate a limited fund to the team leader as per the budget or profit. The task of the team leader is to distribute this fund among team members. Will each team member get the same amount of money? No. Then, how will the team leader decide whom to give the reward and what amount of money? Some might say that all team members must receive the same amount of money. However, this will discourage those who have contributed much better than others, and they may get discouraged in the long run. Those who have not contributed much will think there's no need to stretch as everyone receives the same reward. Such an approach will lead to performance paralysis, and team members would not stretch. So, it is required that performers and nonperformers be identified, and rewards (monetary or non-monetary) are based on the level of performance.

The word for this in the corporate world is the "Bell curve." GE was the first company to use bell curve to rate their employees. Another way corporates do this is by calling it "Allocation of rewards using differentiation based on performance." It is also known as the performance rating mechanism. So here, individuals are to be rated based on their performance. But though the word is performance, many other factors come into play in addition to just performance.

It is not only in organisations but in sports as well. In the Indian Cricket team, which has players on-contract, all players are not classified into one category. Their contracts are in the A, B, and C categories, which the players are put into. The contract money is different for A, B and C.

What I mean to emphasise here is that "differentiation" is always there in some form or another. So, it is natural for an organisation to have a formal "rating system" through their HR. If not formal by HR, the bosses and management must apply an informal way of differentiating its team members. But in a practical sense, both types are applied, formal as well as informal.

What I will do is instead of using various forms; I will use the "bell curve" (Fig 2) as a go-ahead in my illustration.

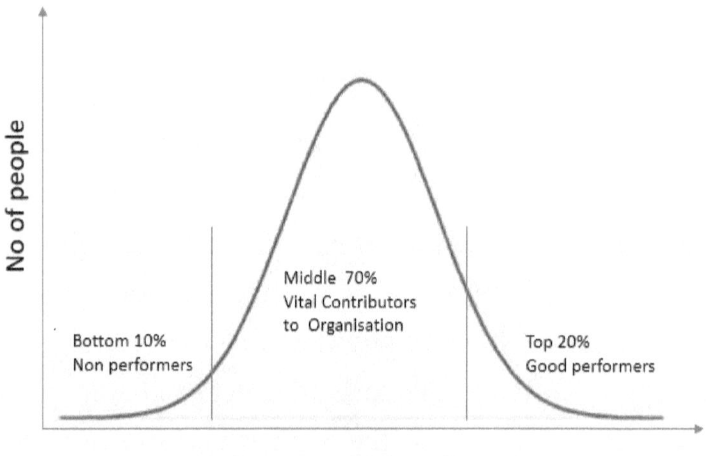

(Sketch is symbolic, not to scale)

Fig 2

A bell curve varies from organisation to organisation.

Some companies employ the "10-20-70 rule," which designates 10% of the staff as "nonperformers," 70% as vital to the organisation, and 20% as good performers.

Some organisations use a ranking system from 1 to 5 with guidelines on the percentage of employees who can be allocated under each rank. (Fig 3)

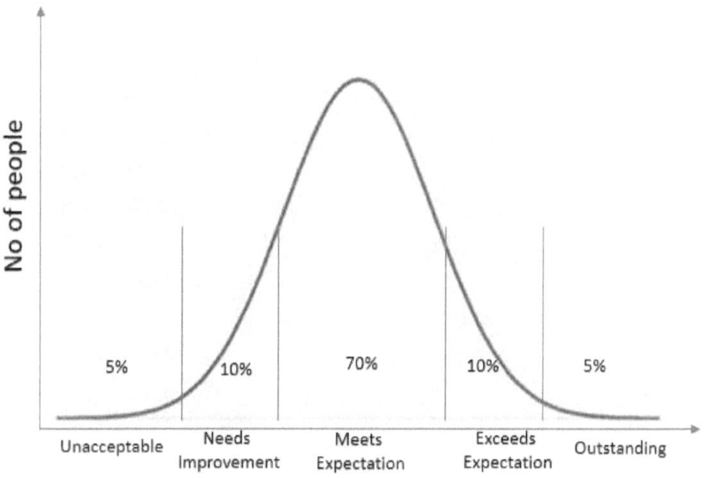

Fig 3

Some organisations have a very clear and symmetrical bell curve. Some tilt the bell curve as per business needs (Ref fitment Table) , with the bottom 5% rated as 1, 10% as 2, 10% as 3, 15% as 4, 25% as 5, 20% as 6, 10% as 7, and 5% as eight. Here, those with rating eight are outstanding, seven being a top performers, six are a top performer, five are vital contributors, four need improvement, and three and below are considered low performers or poor performer.

Bell Curve Fitment Table

% of Employees	Rating	Category
5	1	Low performer
10	2	Low performer
10	3	Low performer
15	4	Need Improvement
25	5	Vital Contributor
20	6	Top performer
10	7	Top performer
5	8	Oustanding performer

They also decide on award amounts and increment amounts for each of these ratings during the annual recognition and reward process. Please note that the reward amount an employee with a rating of eight receives can be significantly higher, often by several times, than what an employee with rating four would get. Therefore, it is extremely important for an employee to be classified as a top or outstanding performer. Now a days, some organisations do relax above percentage limits for each rating class, however overall rating distribution pattern is generally adhered to.

This exercise of performance appraisal and assessment is done annually. Although it is intended to be an annual exercise, as mentioned earlier in this chapter, evaluations by bosses occur regularly and significantly influence the ratings given during the final annual assessment at the end of the performance year. I have also seen few bosses, keeping a log of various events that happen throughout the year so that they refer to it when annual rating exercise happens.

Decisions such as "which employee or team member to assign important tasks to," "which member to place on a team for a strategic assignment," "which member to send to an important customer site," or "which member to ask to present about department/function/organisation activities to an important delegation" are all made on a daily basis according to business needs and therefore occur much more frequently.

While making such decisions, bosses assess an employee's usefulness, even if it is for a specific task as mentioned above. It also indirectly shows the employee's usefulness for the department and organisation.

One may wonder how these assignments matter to an individual's growth or rewards. Many may view them as extra work burden since they are in addition to the employee's regular workload. However, these assignments, first and foremost, indicate that management or seniors see an employee (who has been selected) as having the ability to carry out such important assignments. Just think, when an employee goes to meet a customer or works at a customer site, he/she represent the whole company and must have the ability to make decisions on behalf of the company. Therefore, such special assignments (work) make the employee stand out and help them try out their skills, thereby improving their visibility in the organisation. What we conclude here is that when an employee is selected for such assignments, it benefits the employee, albeit indirectly, in the long run. The question arises again: how do management, seniors, or team leaders select an employee for assignments such as those mentioned above?

Another reason why it is imperative for organisations to have an evaluation system is:

1. If we go back to the organisational structure known as the pyramid form, it is necessary for individuals to advance upwards. This serves as motivation for employees because they know they have a future as team leaders with larger responsibilities.

2. When an employee moves up, the work or tasks which were previously done by that employee will move downwards. Seniors would like to stop doing these tasks to take up the next higher-level tasks.

3. However, these tasks will have to be carried out, and hence they are delegated downwards. So, it is a win-win-win situation. Seniors want to delegate so that they enrich themselves with high-value tasks; management wants to find new leaders who have the ability to do such tasks and also, in the process, identify good and able leaders. As the receiving employee, you get the chance to try and develop many more skills and hone your talent in areas that you are good at—'an opportunity for your development.'

In a nutshell:

1. Evaluation of an individual's performance is a regular phenomenon that happens knowingly or unknowingly.

2. An employee, through conduct and behaviour, helps the leadership and management profile the employee.

3. Gradually, the employee builds an image which helps colleagues and management predict the employee's ability in any situation to carry out an assignment towards organisational goals.

4. Differentiation is key and a widely practised approach when it comes to identifying or picking an employee, be it for promotion, higher responsibilities, performance rewards, etc.

5. Differentiation is applied; it may be in a structured or unstructured manner, depending on the organisation or situation at hand.

6. You, as an employee, keep getting opportunities in a subtle way to showcase not only what you do well but also to learn certain things that make you a better professional.

7. The organisation can keep its vitality, and develop new leaders who bring in new ideas; hence, freshness is in the air.

8. This helps management build a learning organisation / vibrant organisation, which helps employees grow within the organisation.

Even if the evaluation looks like an objective exercise, it has an abundance of subjective components that indirectly have a significant impact on decisions made while evaluating an employee. It is not unrealistic; it is very practical. Even we, as customers, when it comes to choosing a chemist shop, decide which shop to go to based on the Quality of service and the likelihood of availability, even though we know that the price and Quality of medicine will be the same in any shop we go to. This example is used to illustrate that subjectivity has a place in our decisions.

This book is an attempt to classify all such behaviour patterns that have been seen by me, impacting such decisions in various situations in an organisation.

Perception, **Potential**, and **Performance** are the three broad categories under which all these behaviours can be grouped for ease of comprehending the same.

It is common to see employees blaming the system, management, or favouritism by seniors for receiving a low-performance rating and poor rewards. However, one will be surprised to learn that most of these behaviour patterns are under the control of the employee. They are actionable behaviour patterns that can be implemented practically in your daily work life at any moment to achieve a better assessment rating. One just needs to be conscious of these factors and try to focus on them. When employees focus on these factors, it also benefits the organisation because such behaviour patterns contribute to building high-performing, enthusiastic, energetic, and responsive teams, which are the foundation of an organisation that excels in customer response and meets commitments to stakeholders. Ultimately, good employee performance leads to better results at the organisational level. Improving upon these criteria not only helps employees perform better individually but also contributes to building a "high-performing team" for the organisation, comprising of individuals who are strong performers.

Let's begin with **PERCEPTION**:

Is it that truth is truth? Or is perception the truth?

Well, many of us will agree that perception is the truth.

Now, the question is, how is this perception created? One will be surprised to learn that perception is shaped by our own actions—what we do, how we do it, and the way we do things repeatedly. The system, ecosystem, and society (both within and outside the organisation) observe and assess us over time, creating an image of who we are, our capabilities, how we respond, our reliability, and what to expect from us, whether at work or outside of it. The interesting thing is that this assessment often occurs while we are unaware. Please note that our personality is not documented anywhere, but as we progress in life, interact with others, and respond to various situations, we inadvertently make statements about ourselves, and these compile to create an impression for others.

In the following pages, we will explore these behaviours and response mechanisms one by one and see how, within the context of an organisation, these behaviours help to shape our profile and influence our career prospects in the future. You will find these behaviours so simple that sometimes you may be surprised to learn how these small behaviour patterns, when consistently repeated over time, define us to the world, showcasing our strengths, weaknesses, and more.

The first behaviour that contributes to PERCEPTION is **Punctuality** (Being on time).

This is such an underestimated perception parameter that it simply gets ignored by many. Whether it's reaching the office on time, reaching a conference room for a meeting on time, reaching a customer for a business discussion on time, reaching a supplier to discuss material requirements on time, and many more, it is common to blame "other" factors for being late. Seniors blame an earlier meeting or an important call; airlines blame the late arrival of an earlier flight; and many of us, in various situations, blame traffic. We do this to convey that we were delayed due to factors beyond our control. Despite all these factors that would never vanish, if someone keeps appointments and arrives on time not only once but repeatedly, it shows that he/she respects the time of customers/suppliers/colleagues. It shows that you are conscious of constraints (like traffic in this case) and take adequate steps to keep promises (in this case, of time). It shows your respect for the system. The simplest thing one can do is be punctual. I agree that it is difficult but not impossible, and hence, it gets noticed. Be punctual when reaching the office, be punctual when attending meeting, be punctual when keeping a customer or supplier appointment, and many more. Once it becomes part of your personality, you will be punctual even for a family function, for marriages, etc., because it becomes your habit. People see you as "Punctual." People expect you to be punctual.

We, on many occasions, use excuses, but believe me, all these do not work, and in the long run, even these excuses get profiled. It becomes natural to see comments by people about person A, such as "I know he/she won't come in time," and then give the excuse of rain, traffic, a boss's call, etc. When people arrive late to the office in the morning, they reason that last evening or last night they reached home late from work! A justification to arrive late to the office the next day! This once again indicates that you are not putting effort into arriving at the office on time but are taking it as a right not to be in the system by reasoning it out.

The question is how punctuality affects your rating. Does it put a mark on your "commitment?" In this case, what is your commitment to rules? Does it put a mark on your ability to anticipate constraints and manage them to keep your promise?

Let me give you a situation:

The boss had an appointment with a customer at branch office the next day at 10 am to discuss some important subject. The boss was to be out for a meeting in the head office and was expected to be back in the branch office (their place of sitting) by 9.30 am.

However, the previous day evening, boss got a call from the customer that they would reach the branch office by 9.00 a.m. Now, the boss is in a dilemma as to how to keep the customer engaged for half an hour, that is, from 9.00 to 9.30 am. Boss thinks he can utilise these 30 minutes with the customer to talk about the organisation's newly launched digital initiatives and also some new product/solution offerings the organisation is planning to introduce in the next six months. Boss has two people in the team who can do this and are in a position to make a presentation to the customer on these topics. These two persons are Aditya and Pramod. How does the boss decide whom to select? Will this be a selection based on whom the boss likes or who is closer to the boss? The answer is a big NO.

Boss will select the person who can do this job nicely and who will be certain to meet the customer and receive the customer when the customer arrives at the office.

So, what will go on in boss's mind?

Aditya is known in the branch office to be one of the first to arrive at sharp 8.45 am or before. Pramod is late in arriving and invariably reaches the branch office 5 to 10 minutes late. Will the boss take a chance with Pramod or go with Aditya as a sure bet? He would not like to keep the customer hanging in the office unattended!!

The obvious answer is Aditya gets this opportunity to meet and spend time with this senior customer executive who happens to be the Dy MD in his own organisation. So, it was Aditya's past behaviour pattern that profiled him as a sure shot of a timely arrival to whom the boss gave this opportunity. Aditya got an opportunity to meet this senior executive, make a presentation about offerings, answer questions from the customer's side and, in the process, create a new acquaintance, hone his skills, and above all, be in the confident books of his boss. The questions that the senior executives would have asked were for Aditya to handle them and, if not, seek the answers later. This develops Aditya's understanding of the organisation and its offerings.

This is how one gets opportunities, though these are extra work but are also avenues an employee gets to show skills, get visibility and in the process stand out. Who knows one fine day the next job change Aditya is seeking or offered happens to be from an organisation where the same senior executive is in the interview panel!!! Aditya here scores on two front, one in his own organisation and second with a senior executive of another organisation

Another example is when you start working in your function, you will be convening a few meetings to discuss some inter-functional topics; it is for you to show that you ensure that the meeting starts on time and also ends on time. This indicates you value others' time and do not allow the meeting to drift over beyond the allocated time. Even when you are to make a presentation at a meeting or conference, you must ensure that you do not exceed the time allocated and eat away other presenters' time. A simple thing is when you are seeking time from your boss to discuss an important topic and request for a 15 minutes meeting. You must prepare well and ensure that you close the discussion and seek necessary input from the boss within 15 minutes.

Time management is one of the key characteristics of global organisations. Time management will nurture discipline which is a strong leadership Quality.

Let me give you another way to look at time. We all measure life in what unit? Isn't it time?

We say so and so lived for 85 years, so and so's age is 40 years, etc. This unit of year is time, isn't it? The smallest unit is minutes (a practical unit in our day-to-day work). So, if one learns to manage time, life management happens automatically. I remember reading one quote many years ago:

"Even Gandhi, and Nehru had 24 hours." Please note all of us have 24 hours. A CEO, a PM, a shopkeeper, a housewife— all roles have only 24 hours, so how one uses these 24 hours shows how one is using life. Time management, hence, is a very essential skill to go up the ladder.

The next behaviour that forms PERCEPTION is **Appearance** (Visual look).

We all have heard one saying, "What you see is what you believe."

We also have heard that "First impression is the last impression."

Employees must appear enthusiastic, energetic, approachable, neat, and systematic. Many organisations now have a dress code for their employees. If there is no dress code stipulated by the organisation, then one must ensure proper dress, which is a formal but simple dress, in the office/factory. Well-groomed hair, a trimmed beard (if any), polished shoes, and other personal hygiene go a long way in making one look amenable and approachable. It also speaks about how the person is likely to approach work. A neat, well-planned worktable, cabin, etc, all speak a lot about the person and contribute to building an impression. It is seen that in college days we wear many types of clothes, sometimes a new employee may continue this practice even at work which is not correct. One never knows when you are attending office in jeans or did not shave/trim your beard, and as soon as you reach the office, you come to know that today the CEO is coming to the office, and one of the sessions is an introduction to new joiners. One can imagine what impression the CEO will have of you. This was one rare chance, but …. accidentally, you missed it. One may say, Oh, I was not aware, blame destiny, but as it is rightly said, destiny, in this case, was in your hands. Please note it is not only your dress; even the way you stand, sit, the way you listen, the way you walk, and speak are all part of your appearance, and they keep sketching your personality gradually. Good colleges do have special sessions for outgoing students on etiquette, including eating.

A pair of trousers and shirts where the trouser can be of dark shade and shirt of light shade. A good brand requires an investment of around INR 5000. Sports shoes are a big NO in office, a formal shoe is what is expected, and it be cleaned if not polished regularly. Many employees carry a backpack, keep this also in proper shape and not torn etc.

It is easy, and with reasonable spending, one can ensure this. One just has to be sensitive to these points affecting "Appearance."

Appearance is a silent radiator of your personality, conveying qualities connected with work such as :

- You are disciplined.

- You are good at self-management.

- You are systematic.

- You are organised.

- You are happy.

People like to have such individuals around them. They like to work with such people. This enhances your chances of being involved in teams, thereby increasing your participation, visibility, and development.

The next behaviour that forms PERCEPTION is **Accuracy**.

No one likes mistakes. Many people are not aware of this fact. A mistake as simple as a spelling error in emails is not appreciated, even though it may not be related to your work. Some people create slides but texts containing spelling mistakes. In today's world, where MS Word has a spell-check function, this is not acceptable. It shows that you are not serious in your job and cannot ensure error-free messages, emails, or slides. If this is the case, how will you perform error-free tasks? Sales personnel should create error-free quotations; finance personnel should produce error-free financial statements, and production/quality/planning personnel should ensure error-free reports.

I remember once, in my early days in my organisation, I submitted a test report. It was forwarded by someone to our business head as an analysis report on a Quality issue we were facing. Setting aside the results mentioned in the report, the number of punctuation errors I made irritated the boss so much that the report came back to me with him personally highlighting the places where I had made those errors. In those days (not an email era) , the hard copy print of my report came back with his comments.

Mistakes, no matter how minor, irritate others and project a negative image of you. Avoiding mistakes prevents a negative impression. Just imagine if you are perceived as someone who frequently makes mistakes—will you be entrusted with important assignments? The boss may think, "If I assign a task to this person, where will I find the time to check and correct mistakes?"

You just lost an opportunity to showcase yourself to the organisation through an important assignment. Repeated mistakes profile you as:

- Someone unable to concentrate.

- Someone lacking in knowledge.

- Someone careless.

- Someone who does not learn as time progresses.

- Someone who does not respect assigned work.

- Sometimes, it also indicates that the person does not enjoy the work.

The next behaviour that forms PERCEPTION is **Responsiveness**.

This is a huge indicator of your personality. It is said that the biggest expectation people have these days from anyone is responsiveness. This applies not only within the organisation or business circle but also across other fields. Responding is a simple and easy yet uncommon thing.

We, as customers, always expect a fast response.

'No response' in today's world is suicidal behaviour. Numerous customers are lost simply because service or product providers have not responded.

Take a simple etiquette of mobile telephone calls. See what happens.

During our discussions, don't we label a person? Saying, "Leave it, she/he won't pick up the call?"

"Do not worry even if she/he did not pick up the call, she/he might be busy, she/he will call back!"

The situation is the same in both cases—the call was not answered. However, in the above two scenarios, we use different labels. How do we know this? It's based on the behaviour we observe repeatedly in different individuals. If we do not pick up calls, we demonstrate what type of person we are. If we pick up calls or call back immediately, we demonstrate what type of person we are.

Now, how does this matter in an organisational scenario? An organisation is where teams work together to achieve certain goals/objectives; hence, every team member must contribute.

'No response' labels a person as non-reliable. For example, if Aditi seeks help from Prameela:

Scenario 1- Prameela can respond, stating she tried but was unable to obtain the information Aditi asked for.

Scenario 2- Prameela promises to do something and then remains quiet and does nothing, neither goes back to Aditi.

In scenario (1) above, Aditi did not get the help she wanted, but this is much better than "no response." Aditi understands that Prameela may also have limitations, but if Prameela does not respond (scenario 2) then Aditi feels ignored, and Prameela gets labelled as non-supportive and non-respectful. This will hamper Prameela's chances of being selected for a team when it is being formed and members are being picked.

Responsiveness is one Quality that brings energy into the team, making them a "can-do" team. Hence, leaders look for members known to be responsive in their behaviour. Again, if one gets a chance in team selection, he/she gets an opportunity to contribute, become known to many, demonstrate his/her skills, and stand out.

Some Do's and Don'ts in this area can be:

- Decide that all missed calls in the day will be answered by evening, if not immediately, even after office hours are over.

- Decide that all emails will be replied to/responded to within 24 hours, if not by the end of the day.

- Keep a response/promise card, which is different from a to-do list. This card will have a few entries reminding you about whom you need to respond to regarding the help they sought. Note that the to-do list includes many tasks that you have planned to do, but the promise card has those task elements that others are expecting from you because you have promised them.

Emails have the provision of delayed delivery; use this to remind yourself of any promises you made to someone that need to be completed after a week or a month. The email will come back to your inbox and appear as "Unread." Once you open it, it will serve as a reminder.

Have a practice of responding even if the work is not yet completed by the promised date. This signals to the other person that you value their request, and before they remind you, you have already informed them that the work is in progress and may take some more time.

I would like to give a real-life example here:

I had two subordinates, Shashank and Mihan, and my boss and I were discussing annual rewards. It was obvious that these two were being compared to decide who was better between the two. My boss rated Shashank lower than Mihan, and when I inquired about the reason, he cited the difference as:

He said (and I quote), "Shashank, when I give him any work or task, I will not hear anything, and one fine day, I may have to remind him about it. But when I give a task to Mihan, I am rest assured that Mihan will do it. And in case it is getting delayed, Mihan will come and tell me that he needs some more time to complete the task."

A good idea can be all emails in your inbox are seen as "read" so they are not bold. Either you have read and deleted them, read and set for delayed delivery because you are going to work for a few days, or given the decision the email was seeking and then deleted. It is good to keep as few emails as possible where you do not need to scroll through your inbox. This practice can be done weekly, if not daily, depending on the number of emails you receive in a day.

Consider a boss-subordinate situation:

A boss generally has more than one team member. Imagine a situation where Boss Arvind has given Aditya a task to complete a certain assignment. A time target may or may not have been given. Now, it is likely that Arvind may not remember this or may even forget it. Aditya has two choices: he also forgets, thinking that Arvind (Boss) will forget as time passes. Another choice is Aditya, takes this as an opportunity to work on an assignment where he does not have a timeline and hence can do it as and when he gets time and completes the assignment.

Now, one day, Arvind finds himself in a situation where he comes across certain issue and suddenly remembers that the assignment he had asked Aditya to complete is urgently needed. So it is obvious that he will ask Aditya about the status of that assignment:

If Aditya had not completed it, thinking the boss might have forgotten, Arvind will carry the impression that even though he gave the assignment to Aditya, he did not do it, and Aditya is not a reliable team member.

But if Aditya had already done it, Aditya will score, as Arvind will carry the impression that even if he had not followed up, Aditya has done the job. Aditya is seen as a member who does not need follow-up. A great trait for being professional.

Over and above, imagine if Aditya had gone back to Arvind, even without Arvind following up, saying, "Boss, the assignment you had given is completed!" Aditya will be seen as an employee who does not need follow-up.

In certain situations, the boss may not specifically give a task but may mention his/her desire for a certain activity to be done. Here, as well, if one has the habit of noting such remarks and working on them, it helps if such remarks are acted upon and the boss is updated once completed.

The response has a huge impact on building one's image, and whatever effort is put in to enhance one's image is less, as 'Response' is one area where expectations are on the rise (especially due to the availability of technology), and examples are all around which further educate people to think what they expect in response is feasible. Top leadership, if seen as responsive, impresses the staff and the general public. If many of the employees are responsive, it becomes organisational culture. These days, the response can be a differentiator in business. However, the same cannot happen unless more and more employees have this trait. For example, Amazon – look at the details they keep updating about the status of orders, and look at their refund mechanism. It has zero people contact but works well and quickly. Look at Domino's delivery system; it keeps informing you about the status of your order. Please note that updating information shows not only your response to how much importance you give to a customer's order but also raises faith in you, and you become a dependable employee/organisation. An organisation is how its team members/employees are...

Another dimension of response is the speed of response. Response given is welcome and if it is given fast that adds flavour. Many times response is given but given much later; it is as good as 'no response.' It is good practice to ask the time target while accepting an assignment or accepting someone's request for information or help.

Being responsive profiles you as:

- One who respects others.

- One who is committed.

- One who is organised.

- One who is mindful of others.

- One who is customer-oriented.

- One who is in control of his/her work.

The next behaviour that forms PERCEPTION is the **Positive approach** (one that always shows expectancy).

"Leave it, yaar, if I go-to him/her, he will only say negative things and spoil my mood." Do we all not come across this sentence occasionally? In this world, which has a lot to discourage you, one looks for avenues wherein they can get some positive vibes, and one looks for shoulders whereupon

they can download their worries and get some positive outlook about their issues. Team members like to prefer positive thinkers unless the person has a certain skill, which is rare and is a specialisation.

A positive thinker gets more opportunities either in teams or to lead projects and/or to represent the organisation. This puts you in the forefront and helps in your visibility. Remember, more opportunities mean more avenues for you to learn and develop yourself. More opportunities mean more skill enhancement possibilities. After college studies are over, how does one learn? It happens only at work and hence it's good to have more assignments.

Reasons why positive thinking helps:

- People enjoy working with you.

- Teams have tasks to do; a positive thinker brings a can-do approach within teams.

- People approach a positive thinker if they need help or want advice, as they are sure they will get it.

- You become a "go-to" person in the organisation.

- A positive person automatically becomes an energetic individual, which makes you seen as a contributor and hence wanted by many, be it bosses, colleagues from other functional areas, members of your own function, your customers, suppliers, etc.

Being positive profiles you as:

- A "can-do" type of person.

- A motivator.

- A team player.

- An optimistic person.

- A person who fills energy into others.

The next behaviour that forms PERCEPTION is **Interest**.

The amount of interest you show in any assignment or work assigned to you.

In India, there is a saying where phrases used are:

- *"This painting is made with heart."*

- *"Yeh Kaam Dil se Kiya Hai." (This work is done with heart.)*

- *"The fellow puts his/her heart into work."*

- *"Whatever he/she does, does with his/her heart."*

- *"Bahut bareeki se kaam kiya hai." (A lot of detailing has been done.)*

- *"Every minute detail is kept in mind and has been taken care of."*

We all know the difference between automatic tea and homemade tea. A homemade tea and a tea poured in an aircraft or tea from a vending machine (all have the same ingredients but taste is a huge difference).

Many restaurants are now putting stations during breakfast, which they call live counters. Here, you can get proportion of ingredients in the food as per your need while asking for tea, paratha, dosa, etc.

All the above shows that more interest, more involvement in anything makes it better in Quality and hence it is noticed as well as liked. Isn't it home-made tea the best?

But the question is how one can make out if the job is done with heart! Such assessment, how can one make it? A big question??!!! Isn't it?

Answer: Your work shows all these. Your work output is a canvas of how much heart you have put in. Your work shows whether you have done the work with interest or just done for the sake of doing it.

Someone who simply keeps a set of documents on the boss's table for perusal. Are documents arranged in order so as to help the boss logically go through them and make a decision?

When you present your work to others, when others observe the output of your work, it is a huge indicator of your personality.

I will give you an example:

Many times people write emails and end it by writing the word "Regards" as "regards" or "Rgds."

I take it as casual or even disrespectful if you do not have time; then it's better not to write the word "Regards" instead of writing a short form of the word. Do not show "Regards" if you cannot write it in full or do not have time to write it in full! Yes, SMS writers would not agree with me, but at least in emails/messages which are for business purposes, the short form is just a big NO.

Let me give you a real-life incident which happened in our office a decade ago:

I was in a department which had been given a special assignment of getting the organisation certified under ISO 14001. Our department head was leading this initiative and was heading a team of various functional representatives. They had also hired an external consultant who used to visit us on a regular basis to guide us.

One day, during one such visit, the consultant was sitting inside the cabin with my department head, and my colleague named Gopi, who was a coordinator and was assisting my department head in this, was also inside the cabin with the department head and the consultant. Suddenly, the consultant wanted a set of data/information to be compiled onto one page so that it becomes easy to refer to when given to the teams. The consultant asked Gopi if this compilation could be done. Gopi, not so expert at computers, told the consultant that he would ask one of his colleagues, who is very good with computers, to try it out.

Gopi came out of the cabin and approached his team member, Droop, for help. Please note that Droop had no direct involvement in ISO 14001 and had no formal assignment under ISO 14001. Because Gopi, his colleague friend, had asked him, he decided to try doing the compilation. By evening, he had succeeded in compiling the same in one single page and had handed over the final summary (one page) to Gopi.

Gopi took this inside the cabin and gave it to the consultant. When the consultant saw the work, his response was: He asked Gopi: "Who did this work?" Gopi replied that one of my colleagues did it!

The consultant said: Tell your colleague if anytime in life he needs work for whatever reason, he can approach me; I will be happy to have him in my team!

Now, let us reflect on this incident: here, the consultant never met Droop. What travelled from Droop to the consultant was the work done by Droop. The consultant just looked at the work, and it spoke so much about Droop's capability and methodology that the consultant was able to profile Droop as a person whom the consultant would like to have in his team/ organisation. Your work manifests your personality.

As we saw in the example of making tea, a good tea and a bad tea will have the same ingredients, but the process of making it determines its Quality. A Quality job requires involvement, and that comes when one puts one's heart into it. The point here is to note that a person who drinks tea may not know how to make a good tea but knows how to judge a good tea. So, the output of your work gets assessed instantly and helps profile you as an employee, a worker, or a team member.

It is not only the output but also the way you carry out your assignment that tells if you are doing it with interest or doing it as just one more "task" given to you.

So, the learning is to do the work with interest, give it everything, and use it to showcase your personality; one never knows what will click and where , when this "work" may turn out to be a game changer in your job journey.

Doing work with interest profiles you as:

- Someone who loves what he/she is doing.

- Someone who knows the job well.

- Someone who has the skills to do a job well.

- Someone who respects the job and also the customer to whom the job output will reach.

- Someone who is Quality-minded.

The next behaviour that forms PERCEPTION is one of a **helpful nature**.

People are always looking for help, be it guidance, support, advice, or information.

Let me cite a real-life situation:

When we enter a bank and are seeking some information or need help to do our work, we do not know anyone but assess the faces of the staff there to make an assessment of who will help us. It is very difficult to describe how we decide this, but what is important here is that we are trying to decide whom we approach so that we will get the help we are seeking. And we approach that person. Even in an office scenario, the same thing happens; people come to us because they feel we normally help and we have the ability to help them with the problem they are facing.

This works in many ways:

- The person (who is seeking help) solves his problem and eases his situation through your help and hence will remember that you had helped him.

- He may even let others or his boss know that you had the ability to help him/her come out of a complex situation.

- He keeps gratitude towards you which is kind of your emotional bank balance with him for further encashment. One never knows when you may be needing help, and he is the person who will be the one who can help you.

- You are seen as "a person to go-to" within the organisation.

- The fact that you get a situation which you simplified, your skill gets enhanced as in the process of solving his/her problem or guiding him/her you hone your skills further.

- The more people come to you for help, the more you become a person whom no one will refuse to help tomorrow. Please note that in an organisational scenario, mutual help is a must; otherwise, teams will fail if members do not cooperate with each other.

Last point above makes your job easier, so in your own assignments, you find others helping you and not refusing to help or giving excuses as to why they are not in a position to help. Many times, people give excuses not because they cannot help; they give excuses just because they do not want to help. If they want to help, they go out of their way to help.

I will remind you here of a situation which I am sure you would have come across:

Person A goes to person B seeking some information; person B cites some urgent assignment with a timeline, where B is busy and hence not able to help A.

Now, person C goes to person B seeking almost similar information; person B, though busy with an urgent assignment, answers C: "How can I refuse you!? I will help you, but give me a day or come in the evening after office hours; I will stay back and pull out the information that you want from me?!"

Now, let us reflect here: Person B is the same; person B is in the same situation; person B is being asked the same information. Why was A refused? However, C has been granted the request. It is the image of A and the image of C that person B carries. A is a person who normally does not help others, but C is a person who helps others. It can be said that in the past, when B wanted help, A did not help, but person C had gone out of the way to help person B.

A school of thought is: If you help others, then more and more people will come to you for help; this will load you more. Your workload will increase. Please remember you are in your formative years in the organisation; the more people come to you for work, the more you hone your skills, the more you come to know people, it increases your acquaintance, it increases your fan following, and it also enhances your ability to seek support from others as people, even if they are genuinely busy, will find time, will take time out to help you in your assignment as you become a person who cannot be shrugged off or refused.

It increases your emotional bank account amongst colleagues in the organisation. Bosses are able to spot employees who have a good rapport with others, especially in other functions, and try to use this to get work done on the organisation's objectives. Such people will get more scope to work in teams as they will be an easy pick due to their ability to get a good response from other functions, colleagues, customers, etc. Such people become "Resourceful employees" or "Useful employees."

You will be realising by now how simple behaviour patterns displayed by you on a daily basis are slowly building your brand in the organisation.

It works in your favour in the long run to have more work than no work. We all have read the proverb that one only uses 10% of potential, so there is scope for adding another 90%, isn't it?

In your younger days, you are full of energy; you have a hunger to learn more; you need to practice the theory that you learned in college; you are not burdened with too many family responsibilities, so more work hours, more work assignments will sharpen your saw more as you are a raw material which needs processing to bring out many unknown skills of yours which even you sometimes may not be aware of.

Once we are out of college, work is the only canvas where we learn and manifest who we are.

Helpful nature profiles you as:

1.   A "Go-to" person.

2.   A person who is generally acceptable.

3.   A wanted person in teams.

4.   A popular person.

The next behaviour that forms PERCEPTION is that of a **team player**.

It is said that an *organisation is defined as a place where a set of individuals come together to achieve a financial goal.* We all know that organisations have various functions. Each function has people who carry out roles of functions that they are in. However, for the past few decades or so, CFTs (cross-functional teams) have become very effective and, hence, popular. This is a need as organisations become bigger in size. I remember reading in one of the annual reports of WIPRO that its chairman said: For WIPRO to win, its customers must win, and for its employees to win, WIPRO must win. Taking this philosophy forward, for an organisation to be a high-performing organisation which can satisfy all its stakeholders, its teams must be high-performing ones. Teams become high-performing ones if and only if they have members who have high abilities and skill sets and are also excellent team players. CFTs came into being because it was seen that functions traditionally form silos, and a project/assignment which normally would need contribution from more than one function may get into trouble due to these silos. CFTs were very effective in speeding up the project implementation and target completion.

CFTs foster concurrent working as well, which also slashes cycle times.

We have numerous examples in history where a team comprising of very talented individuals did not become successful, but a team with individuals with average skill sets but excellent teaming abilities have got success. Now, the dilemma is an employee is looking at his/her individual performance and visibility. He/she gets a chance to work in a team that has organisational goals/objectives to achieve. It cannot be that the employee succeeds and becomes a hero, but the team fails in its project. It's like an operation successful, and the patient dies.

Take the example of the Indian Cricket team. Virat scores a century in four out of six matches in the World Cup, but India fails to reach the Finals. Mohammed Shahid is a very good dribbler in hockey, but the Indian team fails to reach the Finals. How will this look? It is anyone's guess. Hence, the teams that you are a part of must succeed before anyone notices your performance. There are many leadership training programmes which run a module on team management. Team members may have team dynamics, and as a team member, you will have to overcome such constraints (you hone your interpersonal skills in the process), but a team player is what gets noticed because he/she not only ensures own performance but also supports, guides, those in the team who are struggling. Companies, while hiring, specifically look for this trait in a candidate.

Look at the 1983 World Cup victory; there were hardly any stars in the team, but collectively, the team won the Cup. Teams succeed not just because they have good members with excellent abilities; teams perform because those good members coordinate well, cooperate well, and become cohesive, with each member contributing their bit, ultimately making one plus one equal 11 and not just two. You might have seen many examples in lawn tennis tournaments where the doubles champions are not necessarily champions in singles as well and also vice versa. So, teaming well requires certain skills, which, if you have them, then you are seen as a good team player, and you also get a sense of fulfilment because your team does well, helped by your contribution.

What are the qualities of a good team player?

- Takes everyone on the team along and never makes it an individual success.

- Tries to help others in the team, if they are lagging, even if his/her own task is completed.

- Always talks about the team's achievements outside, not his/her individual achievements.

- Gives every person in the team a chance to share their achievements.

- Ensures every team member is comfortable discussing their issues or seeking help..

- Places team requirements above their own priorities. A classic example is Rahul Dravid: He kept wickets, opened the batting, batted at number 4. All this was done as per the needs of the team, though he is known as one of the best No. 3 batsmen in the world. A good team player is ready to take any role, any assignment as needed by the team and for the team.

- A team player has a high level of acceptance within the team.

Please note that it is a contradiction to seek individual success but also be a good team player. When the team wins, individual wins have more flair, but if the team loses, an individual might have performed well, but this performance loses sheen. The corollary is if team members do well individually and also coordinate well, then there is a high chance that team objectives will be met and the team will do well. Once team objectives are met, there is positivity all around, and individual performers also then come to light and stand out as great contributors to the team's/ organisation's objectives. So, for a performer, it becomes a win-win situation.

An individualistic approach makes the team fall short of its objective most of the time, and then those who limit their contribution by having individualistic aims in mind do come to light and get a bad name. So, the trick is to unfurl oneself and see to it that all engines are fired and a great amount of coordination is done so as to meet team objectives. A good team player does the same. There can be cases where the function that the team member represents has certain guidelines that the team member may have to comply with. The situation becomes complex if it contradicts what the team is asking for. A good team player will bring in a good balance between the two. This is where concurrent working sometimes comes in. An example is supposing a part or software has to be approved before it is to be tried out in the final product sample. So, the team member who comes from the Quality function must ensure that tests are done, and then only that part or the software can be put into the final product; this series of actions may add to the timeline and may delay the final product completion. Here, an option for the team member from Quality is to mark the part or software that goes into the final product and do the part or software testing concurrently. By the time the final product gets ready, these part or software test results will also be available.

Being a team player brings higher acceptance to you, which attracts more opportunities to you. It adds to your visibility in the organisation. It also enhances your ability to seek support from others when you or your function needs it.

Who are you?

What is your capability?

What is your utility?

It is to be noted that this universe does not know who you are or what to expect out of you. No one has told them before you arrive as to what you will do, what your abilities are, what you are good at. How will you behave, and what should others expect from you?

It is only your behaviour pattern; it is how you react, how you respond, etc., which decides your personality and profiles you. This gets more and more enforced when you do the thing repeatedly, on many occasions, over a period.

Let me derive a management comparison. We all use the word process. It is said that a process, once stabilised, can be predicted. Similarly, any human being, in normal circumstances, the way he/she behaves, acts, and does it consistently can be predicted.

Take a cricket example: A time came in the career of Sachin Tendulkar, that whenever he came out to bat, people would expect 100 from him! Now, who told the public that they must expect 100 from Sachin? Was it informed before Sachin was born? Was it some divine announcement? No, not at all. It was told by Sachin himself! Surprised? I will tell you how! Sachin did not say it in words, but looking at the way Sachin started scoring consistently, people started expecting 100 every time he came to bat. It was Sachin who told the world, "Expect 100 from me!" In fact, if Sachin scores a hundred, it does not surprise people as they take it as normal Sachin behaviour; they may get surprised if, continuously for 5 to 6 innings, Sachin scores very few runs. If Sachin scores 40, people get dejected and say, "Today Sachin did not play well." Let us take another example: Bhuvaneswar Kumar, who generally bats low in the order, scores 40, then people say Bhuvaneswar Kumar batted well. Here, both scored 40, but in the case of Sachin, it was not a satisfactory performance. In the case of Bhuvaneswar Kumar, it was a commendable performance! Why? This has been communicated by these two players themselves based on their past performance.

Similarly, when we consistently show the qualities above, your colleagues, your customers, your team lead, and your management would expect that from you. You will be profiled as "Punctual," "Responsive team Player," "Positive," "helpful," etc, depending on what all the above you have consistently displayed.

And then, when a team is formed and a member is needed from your function, people will say 'take this person'. He is very active in teams and contributes to teams' success. If customers want help, they will contact you first, saying you are helpful. If your boss needs to select between two able people and nominate for an important meeting, he/she will take you, saying 'you are punctual.' So, these are the ways that naturally get you more varied opportunities and, hence, avenues to make yourself and your work visible to many, in the process, develop yourself.

When one displays the above behaviour, one is more liked, more accepted, more seen as a crucial contributor and is more relied upon. Any organisation, whatever type of industry it might be in, whatever be the situation, would prefer to have an employee like you.

The above also makes you more involved in the affairs of the organisation, which is extremely beneficial to you for your growth, professionally, inside as well as outside the organisation.

The more you find yourself wanted, the more you find yourself involved, the more you will align yourself with the organisation and employees therein, and hence, you will enjoy the task much more, you will enjoy the time spent in the organisation much more. All these silently show up in your behaviour, and you will take more interest in the assignment; the more your work shines, the more your happiness in doing work will be visible, which will be seen as enthusiasm, so it is like cyclic and mutual adding type.

It is observed that involvement brings commitment. So, the more you participate, the more you contribute, the more you are seen as a committed employee. This will be a tremendous tag that you will not only cherish but will also give a sheen to your career.

The discussion above, though sounding simple, is extremely effective and works silently to profile you in your career. It gives management the perception that you are the right person to deliver the results that the organisation expects from an employee. You may be of the view that some of these qualities are unrelated to work; you might say that organisations always look at work. However, it is believed that these qualities enhance your ability to elicit responses from others, create a sound ecosystem around you in the areas you operate, and ultimately help you deliver results.

The fact is that these qualities provide answers to questions like: Why does only A get nominated for training? Why does only B get nominated for teams? Why does only C get a chance to make a presentation on behalf of the organisation to an important customer? Why is only D sent to sites? Why is only E rated high during annual appraisals? The qualities covered in this book so far are answers to these questions most of the time. This is what I have observed while sitting in various performance reviews and rewards meetings for almost 30 years of my near 40-year career after I became a team lead and senior.

It is common for us to attribute failures to fate, politics, favouritism, etc. when we fail to receive satisfactory rewards. But if you check all the criteria mentioned above, all of them are within your control, and none of them is due to fate. You are the master creator of these, and you can achieve them if you are conscious of them and put in the effort. Some may have these as natural traits, but those who do not can inculcate them in their day-to-day activities.

After PERCEPTION, the next 'P' is **POTENTIAL.**

How does an organisation assess the potential of an employee? How does an organisation decide on an employee for a future bigger or higher position, considering it has an element of prediction because management would like to choose the right or most suitable person? Please note that potential is for tomorrow and has an element of probability. So, in addition to the PERCEPTION points described above, more factors or observation points are considered. Let us look at them sequentially.

An employee with potential gets a chance to move up or move sideways in the organisation. When an employee is asked to move sideways, it might be part of a plan to give him or her more exposure, considering his or her potential, and ultimately move him or her up in the organisation.

The first criterion that shows POTENTIAL is **Intelligence**.

This one thing, people may say, is God-given. Some people are very good at reading and grasping things; some people are very good at mathematics; some people have very sharp eyesight, and some people are blessed with a sharp memory... Some people have very good retention power; some have a great ability to grasp complex information. These things may add to a person's intelligence. It can be the natural talent of a kind in a person which will make him or her be known as an intelligent person.

However, knowledge that can be gained can largely balance intelligence if there is a feeling that one is not so good at certain things. Many times, we come across situations where an intelligent person does not go-to the top, but a less intelligent person reaches the top!! So, what are the qualities which enable this? Please note that the purpose here is not to showcase the idea that intelligence is not important. What we are trying to dwell upon is even if intelligence (God-given or by birth) is short in someone, then also other things can be done (which are in the hands of a person) which can counterbalance less intelligence level.

After college, when we join any industry/service, we generally have a belief that "Studies" are over and now "earning "will start.

Let me highlight here that earning starts, but more earning depends on / or continuation of earning, depends upon learning and self-development. When we join a job, we are put into a role: These roles can be customer-facing, like business development or sales! You can gain more knowledge by taking part-time or online courses in sales management and/or customer relations. You might get into a role in the Quality function or data analytics! You may take additional courses in statistics and/or Quality techniques. You might be getting a job role in production! You may take courses in human relations, labour laws, etc. Acquiring knowledge which gives you a broader perspective in the role that you carry out on the job makes you more knowledgeable in that field. You will be known more as a learned individual than an intelligent individual. If you are known as an intelligent and learned individual, it is a best option. However, intelligence, knowledge, and qualification are on paper unless they are put to use. Your job becomes your canvas; try new things and put what you have learned into practice. You see results, then it makes you feel happy and, at the same time, increases your confidence level; the organisation sees you as an innovator, a person who is willing to try new things. The more you try these things, the more COMPETENT you become.

The next criterion that shows POTENTIAL is **Competence.**

Let me reiterate here that intelligence may be God-given, but knowledge and competency are acquired. A person might be intelligent but may not be competent. A person may have knowledge but may not be competent. So, how does competency is acquired? Competency is the sole result of "trying." It has an element of "Training." It has a good number of practical elements. We might be realising that with education word, we do not use the word training, but with skill word, we use the word training. Training makes a person skillful. Practice makes a person skillful. We always see sports personnel doing practice for hours and hours. It all is to train oneself. If one trains well and acquires skills and puts those skills to use, he becomes more and more competent. As our competency increases, we are in a position to deliver results more consistently; the more this happens, the more issues are put before us; the more we resolve them, the more we become competent. So, it is cyclic.

Knowledge and competence in an area make you seen as a "Subject matter expert," and hence, when a representation is needed from a function while forming a team on topic of strategic importance, then generally, the selection is made based on who knows the subject well, and this subject matter expert gets selected. Let me give you an example: Just imagine your organisation is planning to switch over to SAP-based operations. A team that is formed needs people from major function areas like planning, purchase, distribution, logistics, sales, production, etc. Now, the person who will be selected to represent the function will be the one who has many of the qualities mentioned above and is also a subject matter expert. If you are selected, then you get to learn SAP implementation in your functional area, and you get to interact with the consultant's body, which is overseeing/handling SAP implementation. Are you not getting exposed to a future prospect? Are you not enhancing your CV for a better prospect? Are you not becoming more skillful? Are you not becoming more competent in your functional area?

The next criteria which shows POTENTIAL is **"Be in the boss's shoes,"** or one may say **"Ability to replace the boss and take higher responsibility."**

When the word potential is used as an English word, it signifies the future; it signifies if a person has the capabilities in him/ her to take up higher roles, bigger responsibilities, and larger responsibilities, sensitive/strategic responsibilities in future. If we ask this to the person, the obvious answer will be YES. However, the management, as well as the bosses, have to assess, as they are the ones who will take this call and identify a person who has potential. Now, once again, this gets assessed over a period of time during various behaviour patterns that you display. As an employee, you get many opportunities where you can display your potential.

I will cite a scenario:

Imagine a situation where your boss, who also happens to be head of the function (you work in), is on two weeks' leave. This is a very common scenario and can happen in the organisation.

Take a situation where someone from another function contacts you, as he/she has some work with your boss related to your function. Now, one option is to just answer by saying, "Sir, Boss is on leave" he/she, at the most, will further enquire when is boss resuming duties, and with that information, he/she will go back and see how he/she can manage work without the help being sought from your boss/ function. There is no question about such an approach, and in many cases, this approach is normally seen; when one's boss is on leave, and someone is asking for him/her, the reply will be as you gave in this option.

Another option, now read this carefully, is to ask the person as to what work he/she had with your boss. Was it personal or related to your function? If he/she discloses the work he/she had, you try to understand the requirement, and then you offer him/her if some details he/she can provide, and then you will see what and how help can be given. You take the lead and discuss with other colleagues in your department and see if collectively you can respond as per your past experience how your boss would have responded. You can mention that since work shall not get hampered, you will try to do something, and later, when the boss resumes, you will seek his/her approval to keep records as per process. You may say that this was not possible because the work was of the type where the boss needed to be involved. So, you ask this person (seeking help) if it is urgent and something which cannot wait?

If so, then you take all the details from this person and send a message or call your boss (maybe in the evening), appraise him about this person's request and seek direction from the boss. It is possible that the boss may guide you to the next set of actions. The next day, you can appraise this person about the same and ensure that work is not hampered.

Now, when such a response is seen from you, it gives the following messages:

1.   You are willing to take initiative.

2.   You ensure that work is not hampered.

3.   You care for the organisation.

4.   You take responsibility.

Slowly, when such type of events repeat, other functions, even juniors in your function , start seeing you as an alternate in your dept and as and when the boss is on leave or on long-term assignment, they start coming to you.

You slowly / gradually become the unofficial No. 2 in the dept and show to the organisation that you can be a replacement for your boss in case a need arises or a situation calls for it. When you get the confidence of your boss, he/she should get this confidence that you will keep him/her informed and not bypass him/her but at the same time ensure that he/she or your function does not become obstruction to the work/project of importance. The above is possible, especially in today's world, which is full of digitisation.

The alternate view can be, as many times people mention that their boss does not involve them, the bosses always want to be in the loop whenever any communication is outside the function, are scared of their position thinking their subordinate, if involved, may overtake them, etc. Yes, a situation can be as mentioned here. But even in these situations, what was suggested in the second option above will work, maybe gradually. An important point is you must keep the boss in the loop; you must be his confidant. You shall not bypass him/ her. Even if your next superior (boss of your boss) calls you directly for some information or a meeting, as soon as you return, you must appraise the boss about the same so that he/she is always in the loop. Please note that nowadays, good organisations have, at various levels, something known as "Succession planning"; hence, even from an organisation process point of view, there is a need to identify a successor. This identification is to be done by your boss himself/herself. Hence, your above-mentioned approach will increase your chances of getting identified by your boss as a successor.

Will describe another situation: Imagine a visitor arrives at your function, and the person has come to meet your boss. It so happens that your boss is stuck in a meeting with senior management, and that meeting has been extended. I am sure the boss's secretary (if there is one) or someone from your group will ensure a seat for visitor and offer some tea/coffee etc. But if you see a person sitting for a long time, you may interfere and start engaging the visitor in some discussion about their company or your organisation and assess what his/her exact requirement is. There may be a possibility that you may be able to help and, in the process, fill in the time before the boss arrives. One option is you may make a presentation about your organisation/function to this person. Now, what will happen when your boss arrives? Boss will see you taking this initiative and doing part of the work which boss anyway would have done.

This is another indication that you can be successor to your boss. You not only gain his/her confidence but also make an acquaintance with the visitor person, as he/she will realise that you took the initiative and ensured that his/her wait time is not wasted fully. So, you will have to sniff avenues where you can fill in your boss's shoes depending on a situation and demonstrate to the organisation that you can take higher responsibility. Please note that organisations look for role enhancement and role enlargement as part of their people development plan when it comes to promotion from one grade to another. Every promotion leads to a change in designation and, above all, an increase in remuneration sooner or later. I always say this is where you grow in the organisation vertically. Much more on this when we come to the CAREER section in the later part of this book.

So, making boss redundant, in a way, is an indicator that you are ready for higher position. This comes when you can do the boss's work.

One more example of how you can start thinking or looking at things the way your boss does: Imagine you are leaving the office, and for the past few days, *you invariably see your boss sitting late. It may be a good idea to peep in and enquire if you can be of some help to your boss. Sometimes, the boss may ask you to compile some information or data which he/she needs as a backup for his/her meeting with top management. Sometimes, the boss may ask you to prepare a few slides, which can be inserted into his/her overall presentation.*

Please note that this is not sheer work or helping hand, when you do such a thing, the interaction that you will have with your boss will give you insights into how seniors think and deal with a problem. It will broaden your perspective and help you in enhancing your potential.

There is sometimes the role of substitutes in sports, politics, and even in organisations where you, (if not officially appointed caretaker for a time period or otherwise), can make this additional job as an opportunity to portray your potential to the organisation. You have to grab this opportunity by taking the initiative and doing that extra, stretching extra for your own benefit in the long run.

The next criteria which show POTENTIAL is **Communication**:

Wherever you work in India, English being widely used in the organisation, you must be able to communicate in English. It is not mandatory, but it helps a lot if you are able to speak English. Organisations communicate in English. Meetings, emails, etc, all happen in English. So, you must be able to write and speak good English. Remember, we are still on the topic of your perception and potential. So, what do you talk about? How do you talk? It gives an impression of how you think. What do you think? Yes, in the initial weeks/months of your joining the organisation, you will get a chance to attend meetings and group discussions: you may listen and grasp issues and observe how solutions are offered and decisions are taken. However, one day will come when your organisation would like to have your contribution to various issues and objectives. Here, your communication ability will help in the following:

1.   Offer clean insight into solution being offered by you.

2.   Indicate how objectively you think.

3.   Indicate your ability to do strategic thinking.

4. Your ability to articulate clear thoughts.

5. Your ability to influence others.

The above (5 points) help profile you and influence others about your potential. Please note that you may think many things, but if you are not able to articulate them, you will lose a lot in the long run professionally. While English is a medium inside an organisation, with customers, suppliers etc. Roles such as Govt jobs, banks, even sales do require additional proficiency in local regional language.

In fact, knowing a regional language will not only enable your own job execution, but sometimes, you may be a medium used by your seniors in situations where they find themselves lacking communication ability in the local language.

How does one develop these skills? Listen to good lectures on YouTube and enrol in good online courses. Enrol for the course in "presentation skills." Please note that it is not only speaking good English and/or correct English, but it is also putting your points/thoughts across in team meetings to seniors while making presentations. Communication is a behaviour which not only speaks about your potential but also impacts perception as the moment you start speaking, you start creating that "impression" we spoke about in detail earlier in this book on "Perception."

While making your points, use the following:

1. Refer to quotes.

2. Use of data

3. Examples from your earlier experience

4. Suggesting in actionable words and small sentences

5. Offering help in trying your suggestion if the organisation finds it valuable.

6. Proposals you make must cover their impact on broader aspects such as Legal, Social, feasibility, financial, environmental, customer image, employee morale, and organisation culture as applicable. This shows your ability to think in totality including types of risks involved while looking at an issue and suggesting solution.

The points above will profile you as a person who is well read, has insight into the problem area, talks solution and not excuses, is a doer and not mere preacher.

After PERCEPTION and POTENTIAL, the next P is **PERFORMANCE**.

You might be wondering when we are on the topic of performance appraisal and performance reward, why this word performance is coming after so much discussion! The answer is that performance appraisal has an objective portion (which is a crucial portion) that is judged by how much of the set targets have been achieved by an employee. However, it has other aspects which we have discussed so far. PERFORMANCE is a necessary and important criterion, but it is not the only one. We will elaborate on it.

PERFORMANCE is generally taken as **Result**. Result is extremely important. Many a times when we refer to a person, while referring to the strength we use the phrase "result oriented person." Generally, in an organisation, the result that you deliver depends a lot on how much support you are able to garner from other individuals, other functions, customers, suppliers etc and for that the behaviour patterns that I have referred to earlier in this book play a key role.

But I would like to add one more aspect, which is **Effort**. The result is what is seen as a performance. However, effort that is put also plays its part when performance is judged, especially when the result falls short of the target or expectation. Even if the result is 100% or exceeded, the good organisations still assess how the same was achieved, how much was achieved, and what kind of effort was put in. The process followed is also on the radar even if the result is met or exceeds the target. While putting in the effort, you have various options, such as trying the theories that you have learned in the past and seeing if you find them working in a particular situation; you can take guidance from some seniors and see what they would have done in such a situation. While you do these things, in case your direct senior (boss) or their senior has suggested something, you must try it without fail by giving it full. If it works, you not only solve your problem but also demonstrate to your boss that their idea worked (happiness to them), and simultaneously, you send them the message that you are obedient.

While you are trying to work around issues, you should not be seen as someone who is giving up early but must be seen as someone who is trying even some out of the box solutions. Your assertiveness will be visible.

The famous commentator, Mr Harsha Bhogle, has a lecture video in which he once spoke to IIM students. He mentioned passion, preparation, and performance. We all know how athletes and sportsmen prepare. It is the effort they put in. I remember, before an ensuing tour of India to Australia, how Virat Kohli was toiling it out under the Sun for 8 hours. He was making his body fit enough and enhance his stamina to play long innings. He knew that his performance result may be affected not because he was short of skill but due to a lack of stamina which he may find affected by the weather conditions out there. So, in any task you get, yes, the result matters, but effort also matters. And the effort has preparation as part in it. The interesting point here is that the world knows, your organisation knows how you are preparing, what effort and how much effort you are putting in. We all know the phrase "well played" is used for the losing team if their effort is commendable but the outcome is the unsatisfactory result.

Passion to perform scores far higher than ability. Ability opens the first door and may open the second door, but not the last one.

If the result is **what**, which is the outcome, and then the effort is **how** the whole thing is being done. How much effort is being put in? The effort shows your preparation, your struggle, your ability to identify future constraints, and your ability to foresee issues and tackle them. It basically shows your attitude. Taking a clue from Cricket: Many times when India loses a match, two types of reaction may come: 1) No one put up any fight, we threw our wickets away, etc. This is a very damaging reaction as it shows that the team played short of their potential. 2) We fought hard; we played better than our potential, but still, we lost to a team which played better than us. This would give the result some respect/ acceptance even if we lose the match.

I would derive another example from the Olympics. Here, in many track and field events, we are generally aware of the potential of our athletes, which also gives a kind of indication about their medal prospects. Now, these are past data, which shows the potential of an athlete. But that athlete in the next Olympics has to repeat that performance or, better it, if a medal has to be won. Now look at scenarios: 1) Athlete fails to win a medal; it is disheartening if the athlete clocked less than his/her potential (past performance) 2) Athlete fails to win a medal. Here, it is not disheartening if an athlete did better than his/her past records (potential), but other athletes did better than our athletes. 3) The athlete wins a medal and has equalled his/her past record 4) it is much more heartening if the athlete betters his/her past record and also wins a medal.

You can see in the above four points:

In (1), the result was bad, but the effort was also bad. In (2) result was bad, but efforts were good (3) The result was good, and effort was also good (4) The result was good, but at the same time, effort was further good.

Think over on the above four situations and you will be able to get an idea why effort plays key role in how organisation looks at you even if result is not as per target. Remember result may not be fully in your hand but effort is in your hand.

I would like to give an example of our triple jump athlete, Dipa Karmakar, who came fourth in the Rio Olympics 2016. She did not win medal but got lots of accolades, which normally only a medal winner gets. Reason is she improved her past performance in Rio Olympics however other athlete did better, hence she moved into 4th position and missed medal

It is important to note here that we all feel that the **result** is what is visible; please note **effort** is also visible. It is visible to others whether you **performed to potential** or below potential.

Would like to bring to your notice that scene in the famous film Sholay, where after the first encounter with Gabbar Singh, Jay and Veeru come to Thakur who is standing by the side near his haveli. Veeru tells Thakur Saheb that they will not work further on the assignment which Thakur Saheb has given them of "catching Gabbar Singh alive." He says they had accepted the assignment because they had seen an Inspector (earlier role of Thakur) fighting with group of dacoits (Gabbar Singh and his men) alone, That effort had given them encouragement as they thought Inspector (who now is Thakur Saheb) is valiant person, but today when they find that Thakur did not pick up a rifle lying in front of him, when Jay and Veeru were fighting Gabbar and his men in Thakur's village, they felt Inspector has now become a coward. Later this film goes into flash back and Thakur narrates how his two arms were cut by Gabbar Singh and hence he did not pick up rifle today.

The above is an example of how effort that you put in, let it be any task, also gets noticed and becomes a useful evaluation criterion in case result is found to be short of target.

It is universally found that efforts bring in result. In the book "Count your chickens before they hatch" by Arindam Chaudhuri, I remember one paragraph, which says "the world stands aside to let pass the man, who knows where he is going." We all hear stories about certain individual building college without having any fund of their own. Even for a bad task, once you have clarity you get people to do it for you. So, all this, what it means? Once again it shows if you are clear in your purpose, if you are clear in what you want to do, then you get support / resource . The constraints should not deter you. Look at how a river flows, if a stone comes in the way, it takes different route, changes path but keeps flowing. Similarly, your efforts should not stop.

Even take customer supplier relationship. Suppose your customer has expected certain things from your organisation and has asked you to help him/her out in this. Now the result may be in the favour of customer, or it may not be. The point is, customer will know how much effort you are putting, in getting his request through for a favourable outcome from your organisation, He/She also knows your limitation due to your position etc, but he/she will appreciate the fact you did put effort equal to or more than your potential / authority even if the result was not in his/her favour.

One more unique relation between effort and result is consistency of effort. In Hindi, there is a saying "Koshish karne walon ki haar nahi hoti." Effort when put consistently in the right direction, one day gives result. Here right direction means, right method, right process etc. When we join industry, we get training on methods we must follow to do our work and get result. This can be: How to engage with customers? How to involve workmen? How to design a product / service? How to attend a service call? How to steer a project? How to procure an item? What we do is we at times don't follow the process and hence result is not seen. These are time tested methods, which are also termed as basic things that must be done to get desired outcomes. These basic things being simple in nature, we do not have faith and hence ignore. Following basics is more connected with sincerity but expertise gets connected with doing things smarter way and this leads to diversion from basics. Basic things must be done in smarter way not either or.

An example: Do accidents happen when we are learning driving, or it happens when we think we have become expert in driving? Most of the time it happens when we think we are expert. Why it happens then? Because then we deviate from basics. While learning we always follow basics like giving signal, speed control, etc.

There is an interesting video of eight min on YouTube. Search it as "Girish Karnad the monk." This is to prove how consistently pursuing right process fetches result.

Effort put sincerely, following basics that is taught, in most cases sooner or later will show result.

In the above discussion if we can make a check on all the behaviour we all spoke about, we can classify each of these to check if it is in our hand or not?!

Here we see each of them and whether it is in one's own control.

Attendance – We are responsible.

Appearance – we are responsible.

Accuracy – We are responsible.

Responsiveness – We are responsible.

Positive Approach – we are responsible.

Interest – We are responsible.

Helpful to others – we are responsible.

Team Player – We are responsible.

Intelligence – God given.

Competence – We are responsible.

Being in boss's shoes - we are responsible.

Communication – We are responsible.

Effort – we are responsible.

Result – This is an outcome where we may not have full control.

Performing to our potential- We are responsible.

So, one of the purposes of writing this book is to drive this fact that many things are in one's own control but generally what we do is blame fate, blame system, blame others … One need to make conscious effort, perform to own's potential, upgrade potential to succeed in this world / in the organisation. Most of the points highlighted above also will give you good outcome even when you apply the same within family, within society at large. They are not only effective in your professional life but equally effective in your social and also family life.

Based on the points made so far in this book and taking forward the three broad areas: PERCEPTION, POTENTIAL and PERFORMANCE, I would now take you to overall message that we derive out of all these.

A. *WORK WORKs.*

This world belongs to doers, and not thinkers: Even thinkers must write or talk (which is an act of doing a book or holding seminars etc) to showcase what their thoughts are to the world.

There is a myth that people go up the ladder due to luck / past tradition. Now we all know the definition of an organisation: where group of people come together with aim of making an economic impact. We also know that organisations are led by leaders at top. Do you think when in an organisation of family managed type, where, say for a while, we assume due to past tradition a family person is given charge at top, however he/she is not performing! What will happen, he/she will not be able to deliver!!! So, the MD has to appoint a competent CEO (System allows it) in order to take organisation to successful performance and create value for its stakeholders. In India's one of biggest industrial house! For the first time in history a non-family person is heading that conglomerate. So, WORK WORKs. I am not saying that favouritism is zero in industry, I am only trying to say that such cases do not last long if the person does not have many of the leadership qualities. So "Apna Aadmi" or

"My person" cases also either develop into a good leader and deliver or today or tomorrow will have to vacate. How many cases like this will be seen around? One day the competent / capable person has to get his chance, deserved by him/her. We also have cases where if a deserving person is not getting chance, he / she gets an offer from competing organisation or different industry. So, work does not go waste, WORK WORKs.

Your next job offer need not be from any job search site. Now a days many agencies map people of certain designation in similar roles cutting across industry, They would hear about you from various avenues in market such as your suppliers, your colleagues, your customers, your channel etc because these are the entities with whom you interact on day-to-day basis and they profile you, evaluate you based on the work you have done for them and/or with them. So, WORK WORKs.

Today, many organisations, while searching for suitable persons for a role, do throw news in market they operate in and try to see if they get recommendations. The paragraph above is highlighting the same. Imagine a multinational, who wants to set up plant in India. They would like to seek employees in various positions . They would find it easy to get tips on who all are doing well, from the ecosystem of suppliers, dealers, stockists, customers, consultants depending on the industry and role.

When you will be interviewed, in case you will try to switch over to a new organisation, please note the interviewer would like to know what all you had done in your job, what new skills you have acquired in various assignments that you have done in different roles. They are trying to hire you for the skills you have acquired, because once you are an experienced individual and are trying to change job, the new organisation expects you to start delivering the next day of you joining that organisation, the interviewer is seeking a readymade person who has the skills that the new organisation is looking for the position in mind. This interview will not be like the interview that is taken, when you had gone for campus placement or which you gave for your first job, fresh out of college because that time the interviewer is trying to ask you questions which relate to your academic subjects and is trying to assess what is your strength subject, how much you know application of the subject that you are good at etc . Your interview, post first job, will have questions from the CV that you have written. Generally, your CV will enrich only if you have worked in various types of projects, in different teams, and have done a challenging assignment. Mere writing number of year of experience will not help. This means that you will have an enriched CV only if you have worked in your current organisation. Hence once again WORK WORKs. You will be able to answer questions to the interviewer confidently only if you yourself were involved in the project / assignment that you have mentioned in your CV.

So once again WORK WORKs. The interview panel is able to figure out level of your involvement, degree of your skills, your ability to overcome constraints by talking to you about an assignment you have mentioned in your CV. Unless you were fully involved, you will not be able to answer and hence will spoil your interview. So once again WORK WORKs.

You get the work what you are good at. I have been telling again and again that the society, the team leads, the people around you keep evaluating you. When they see you doing something well more and more such jobs come your way. There are occasions in an organisation when different events are organised, it may be not relevant to your role/job profile, like annual picnic, Annual get-together, some pooja ceremony, Retirement function, Employee Awards function, customer seminars, etc. There is role during these events which people can take. Roles are like becoming anchor, people can become part of organising teams etc. These things are extra WORK, but they give you opportunity to chill out and freshen up your mind, if you like such roles. They also give you that visibility that I have been speaking about. You are more known, and you stand out. Now when you do such roles well, you get more and more such roles. This is another opportunity for you to innovate in that role and come out better and better each time you do such role. So even though such roles are not directly part of your job, they benefit you. So once again WORK WORKs.

In a normal life of a human being two main phases are:

Phase 1: From birth till age of approx. 22 years.

Phase 2: Life after the age of approx. 22 years

Take any middle-class family, whatever be the financial condition of the family, when a child is born to the parents, they generally try to ensure one thing: They try to ensure that their child goes to a good school. Almost all parents, stretch beyond their normal financial means to ensure that their child studies in a good school. Now why this happens: Why they do not cite examples of a sportsman, film actor who is celebrity and then say, no need to study, still their child can be a successful citizen in this society? This is because, it is generally believed that if one studies good enough till a level, he/she can live in this world in normal manner and can take care of himself/herself as well as their family. So, this means that an individual, keeping exceptions aside, has only one main assignment and that is study till age of 22 years. In social events also, when one meets a youngster of age below 22 years generally the question asked is "What do you study?" I am not here propagating that other than education, no other things is to be pursued. What I am saying is education / qualification helps even in cases where your choice of sports / entertainment etc as a future prospect hits a roadblock. It helps as fallback option.

After 22 years, what is expected from an individual is WORK. Hence the above discussion keeping various aspects in mind on WORK. Because WORK WORKs.

From spirituality angle, WORK WORKs can be said as karma is dharma when you do certain things which is told by your boss. It is dharma for you as you must do it. But how to do it, the way you do it, type of Quality output is karma from your side. While working you may come across an idea on reduction of time, or cost while doing a project. Take that initiative. That is karma from your side.

Say you have been given a task of compiling certain information from the organisations IT system. You complete that assignment but in the process realise that a small software program can be developed which when run as query will throw this information (duly compiled) in less than a minute. This initiative if you take it is Karma.

Let us see one general example:

Take a situation you are driving your car on highway and your car has a breakdown. You sit on sides of the road and do nothing. The passersby will see you and think that "maybe you have asked for help and you are waiting for help to arrive" so no one will stop.

Take another situation, you are trying push the car alone and passerby see you doing this. There is high possibility that someone will stop and give you a helping hand to take the car by side of the road and even help in doing a push start. Only after you do your karma, luck factor may come in.

There is a YouTube video, you may search for it. It is "tum Chalo, Hindustan chale" you will be able to see how a young boy, an incapable person can get a fallen tree shifted from the road and unblock traffic.

Many a times, we find people choosy about work, many a times we find people with view that they would do well in case they get work / job of their choice. This, I will not say is wrong, but I will say it may not happen to all right on day one. And, to some extent it is not in the hand of an individual. So, what you can do is, whatever is the role given to you, excel in it, do it very well. The above criteria applies to every kind of role / job, very few exceptions will be there. As I have been mentioning, in role that you are in, almost all qualities we discussed in this book are noticed by people in the organisation and outside organisation. This only becomes building block for your next opportunity. Generally, what happens is, one gets discouraged in the role if it is not of his/her choice. Such a discouragement affects the way you perform that role. Your unhappiness results in you not enjoying doing the role. Once you do not enjoy doing it, it gets seen by others that you do not do the job well and many of the above criteria you fall short and do not display the same. For examples: You start coming late for the job (Not punctual), You get angry while on job, you do mistakes and repeat mistakes in your work (Not Accurate), you get irritated often (not helpful person) etc. This becomes a vicious circle and negatively affect the chances of any new opportunity which might turn out to be of your liking. This is how you spoil your chances / career/ future. The role that you are in, to your liking or otherwise, is the canvass, where upon what you are is to be manifested, if manifested well it opens door for the next opportunity which possibly can be of your choice, who knows. So once again WORK WORKs even if you work in a role/job which is not of your liking.

It is generally seen that when one passes out from college and is seeking a job in an organisation, one has heard about departments such as production, Sales / Marketing and R&D. However, in an organisation there are departments such as Purchase, Planning, IT Support, Business Development, Quality, Maintenance, Tooling, Production Engineering, Industrial Engineering, Marketing communications, Testing, Project execution, and more. You may get your first placement in any of these, take it and start your journey, keep in mind the points mentioned in this book,

B. *Be valuable:*

All the above points mentioned will help you in increasing value.

This world, the society, the friends, the neighbour, the bosses, the organisation all invariably keep assessing how valuable you are to them. We all have heard one phrase in Hindi" Banda bada kaam ka hai" What it means is this person or that person is very useful asset to have.

You can be a valuable son, you can be a valuable team member, you can be a valuable subordinate, you can be a valuable customer, you can be a valuable supplier. You must have heard about TINA supplier; Here TINA means you become such a supplier that customer will find no alternative to you. You must have guessed TINA means 'There Is No Alternative.' This value makes you stand out, makes you irreplaceable, makes you linchpin and when this happens you are the most sought-after person, obviously depending on the requirement and the role you are in.

The moment you become irreplaceable, your remuneration, your annual rewards, your promotion, your growth in the organisation gets facilitated like anything. You are supported, you are sought after, you are followed. Your fan following in the organisation goes up.

You get to be known to many as valuable employee. Your boss, your function dept would not like to relieve you easily. You become a WANTED person. There are cases when such an employee wants to leave the organisation for better prospects, the organisation makes effort to retain the employee. While making these efforts, enlarged responsibility, higher designation through promotion, promise of salary hike etc in next appraisal cycle, including sometimes even role change is considered. The point I am trying to convey is, when you become a WANTED or Sought After employee, effort is made to satisfy you. Good organisations need good employees. Society needs good people. Family needs good family members.

Take example of a marriage function: There you will find few individuals who are seen running around and doing many activities, they have been assigned many tasks, why? Not because they are liked, but because they are found to be valuable in past with a label that they can do many things efficiently. Their ability to handle crisis, do well in managing complexities, is known. Some people are very loyal to the boss. They are assigned work which needs loyalty, secret things, like keeping confidential documents, etc. reason is they can be relied upon. Some people show good amount of loyalty in exactly following instruction.

Here I will narrate a very crucial incident from the 2007 T20 World Cup.

It was final over and Pakistan needed 13 runs from six balls and one wicket was remaining. The match could have gone any way. Dhoni (the captain) had to choose whom should he handover the ball to bowl the final over. Situation was such that Harbhajan Singh had an over left and could have been the automatic choice. Harbhajan was a lead bowler and specialist bowler in India team. Please note it was Dhoni's first World Cup final and he was not celebrity then in Indian Cricket.

Dhoni wanted the over to be bowled in a particular way. Best thing was Dhoni himself would have bowled that over but being wicketkeeper, he was not allowed to bowl, so he had two options:

Option 1: Dhoni gives the ball to Harbhajan Singh, explains him how he wants Harbhajan to bowl in that over, Harbhajan will nod his head in affirmative. Dhoni goes to his wicketkeeper position Harbhajan walks to his run up. Harbhajan will think, Dhoni's idea will not work, What Dhoni knows, I know more about Bowling. I will be able to get wicket and he bowls his way.

Option 2: Dhoni walks towards Joginder Sharma, explains him how he wants the over to be bowled. Joginder being loyal soldier, understands it well. Dhoni walks to his wicketkeeper position, Joginder goes to his run up and starts the over and bowls exactly the way Dhoni has asked him to bowl.

What are the possibilities?

A) Option 1 is done, and India loses the match. Public would think Dhoni did right thing as he went to his best bowler, so Dhoni does not get blame, Harbhajan gets blame. Here Dhoni would have taken a 'safe' decision.

B) Option 2 is done, and India loses the match. Dhoni takes blame as he did not go-to his best bowler but asked a newcomer to bowl. Dhoni takes risk.

Now, I repeat, Dhoni by that time was not a celebrity whom public will pardon, even if a mistake is found. But Dhoni wanted the job to be done the way he thought. Hence wanted to confirm first that bowler will bowl as per his instruction. If India loses Dhoni takes blame, If India wins, Joginder becomes hero. So Joginder was known to follow what leader will ask, and hence he was selected for this situation.

Same thing happens in an organisation as well, you are chosen for a task because you have demonstrated certain qualities which the job in hand requires to achieve organisation objectives.

C. Do not be choosy, especially in the early days of your journey.

Many times. Employees want a job/project / function of their choice. It might happen that organisation evaluates you in a way where they need your expertise for another project / function. It is advisable that the employee accepts the same and does that role in an excellent manner.

Will give you one example: generally, we will agree that anyone who comes to film industry comes with aim of becoming hero. But in many cases, they get side actor role, or they get villain role. If one believes that he or she is an actor, then he / she must do the role of villain or side actor role also very well. It might happen that the person becomes famous and goes down in history as good villain industry ever had. Or looking at the acting skills the person may get a break in the role of hero as well. But if the person does not do the role given, then door closes for next option.

We come across instances where we see sometimes a very intelligent person does not go-to the top, however an above average person rises to the top. What happens is an intelligent person's intelligence holds the person from giving everything to the opportunity. The intelligent persons keep evaluating the opportunity standing in front: Why this job came to me only, why someone else was not given this job? Or What will I get if I do this job? I am only being loaded with jobs; others who refuse are happy and not loaded more? We never know what destiny has in store for us. Maybe it is this job which may turn out to be a game changer for us, May be the next person whom we meet while doing this job may be the game changer for us?

Will take one simple example of an Auto rickshaw driver. Many a times we find an Autorickshaw driver refusing to come to a destination we would like to go, instead the Auto driver decides to stay unoccupied. The reason driver does so is driver thinks:

1. If this customer destination I go I may not get the next customer and would be idle for a long time or would like to return idle.

2. This customer destination is of a very low fare, so my earning will be less. Better to wait for the next customer sitting idle here, because the next customer will be of high fare or will be going to a destination which will fetch me next customer with higher fare (longer distance).

Now let us analyse this: In (2) above does the Auto driver knows for sure that the next customer will be of high fare or will go-to a destination where the Auto driver's next customer will be of high fare? In (1) above who knows that he takes this customer even if it is of low fare, but the place where this customer releases the Auto, the next customer standing there is a high fare customer going long distance? The destiny is not in your hand, but current situation, how you react is in your hand. Accept current situation, do your best and wait for next big chance. It will come. It has to come! Sooner or later.

D. *"Be the Best" in your role.*

Doing the role may be your dharma. However, doing it in a manner that you become best known for that role is your karma.

We as individual perform various roles. Let me be first very generic: These roles are son/daughter, husband/wife, brother/sister, father/Mother, Neighbour, Administrator, Colleague, Boss, CEO etc. All our effort shall be to be the best in that role: Point here is no one knows what is best. We all think best has come but suddenly a better thing comes and then we think Oh! Best was yet to come and now it is in front of us. So, our effort shall be to be better and better in that role as time passes.

If one has job of a machine operator: How can the person be a best machine operator the organisation ever had.

If one has job of a sales Officer: How can the person be the best sales professional the organisation ever had.

If one has job of a R&D Engineer: How can the person be the best R&D engineer, the organisation ever had.

If one has job of cook: How can the person be the best cook people around ever knew of.

If one has job of teacher: How can the person be the best teacher the school/college ever had.

If one has job of customer executive at a call-centre: How can the person be the best customer executive organisation ever had.

If one has job of project lead: How can the person be the best project lead organisation ever had

These are few examples, and many more can be added.

Let us cite some real-life examples:

Mr E Sreedharan was called as Metro Man of India. He was a professional who was given a task of Delhi Metro project by India government. That time Delhi Metro was first long metro, over ground as well as under the ground in the country to be built by us. He did this job so well, so well that he became known as Metro Man. An example where you excel so much that people start identifying the work with your name.

There are roles in society or in organisation which are generally seen as non-positive or allow me to use the word Showstopper. Like Quality function in organisation, Police Dept in Society, Income Tax officers in Govt etc.

But even in these roles, we come across individuals who not only discharged their duties very well, but also ended up being very popular amongst their peers, other functions.

Take Police officer role: Police officers job is to enforce discipline. Here while doing this, he/she must be strict and also punish those who violate law. So how they be popular? If they are strict, they will not be liked by public, isn't it?

Police officer does not only enforcement of law, but also works on prevention mechanism which ensures non-occurrences of wrong doings. He has regular meetings with public, He/She keeps eye on sensitive occasions where in bad elements may act. He/she keeps a check on bad elements, he /she continuously keeps a communication channel ON with them. Even after so much of effort on harmony and prevention, suppose he/she must finally arrest/punish someone. Public takes it as No option act and supports it.

Similarly, the role of Quality function in an organisation:

The job of Quality professional is to ensure that right Quality goes out to customer. The simple thing that is done to ensure this is after the work is completed, Quality function person will come and inspect. If found not as per specification, the work will be rejected. This is how it is ensured that defectives do not go out to customer. This is traditional method. But here the moment production person comes to know that the work is rejected, there is feeling of loss, no one, including production person wants to send defective work to customer, but loss of time spent, loss of resources spent on the work till now gives that bad feeling.

Suppose Quality professional installs stage wise checks early in the process, the defect might get spotted early in the process and further value addition, resource spent gets avoided. Quality professional can undertake training of operators/engineers to make them aware of right process, type of defects to look for, type of tools gadgets to be used in order to not produce any defective work. This is how the Quality professional not only prevents defects but also upgrades the skill level of the work force. So, the Quality professional does his job of ensuring that defect does not go out to customer, but also generates positive vibes amongst workmen/engineers, production personnel as being helpful so that even resource losses are not seen by the organisation.

I had a colleague in our organisation, named Rajesh. He was for a long time in his professional journey, a Sourcing professional He also led the China sourcing initiative for the business. As part of people development plan, he was given the role of production in charge, with about 100 workmen in his team. He was in production for about three years. Later he moved to another organisation as CEO. Now as per convention he was given send-off by his staff colleagues on the last day in my organisation. The point to be noted here is, he was given separate farewell even by unionised workmen team. Now at least to my knowledge, a send-off to a management personnel by workers, I had not seen. So, see here, Rajesh being in management, is expected to administer discipline, ensure productivity etc from the workmen team. Generally, workmen and management, especially if it is in unionised environment, are on two sides of a table. Even then Rajesh was popular with workmen. He excelled in his role so much that even those who normally are on other side of table, valued his work.

One of the best cabinet ministers in Indian Government is Mr Nitin Gadkari. He is also nick named as highway minister. Why? His portfolio is Road Transport and Highways. He has done such a work while heading this ministry is that the role name is tagged to his name. In the past also many ministers would have headed this ministry, Mr Gadkari would have faced the constraints which earlier ministers would have also come across like, land acquisition, fund availability, technology then how come Mr Gadkari is able to do such an excellent job?! He is the longest serving Minister for Road transport and highways currently running his tenure for almost ten years.

I had one colleague named Naj, in his journey of near 40 years in the organisation his earlier years were in sales and later mfg. was added to his portfolio and he became business head. Right from his sales days, amongst various customers, he was also handling Reliance Industries. Slowly he became Key Account Manager for Reliance Industries and kept increasing the Share of Wallet from this customer. His work, his rapport, his hold with this customer became so intense that a time came, when we used to book 100% of the orders that got released from Reliance. I remember in our board meetings our CFO used to call his name as "Mr Reliance!"

We have numerous cases around us, where we see roles and we see different people in that role at different times. Let us take role of Municipal Commissioner. People come into that role and people go out of that role. Take Prime Minister: 15 people came into this role over past 75 years. Captain of Indian Cricket team: So many players got chance to discharge this role. But how many captains we remember, how many PMs we recollect and recall names in our discussion. How many Commissioners we remember. Why? Some people when get a role, use the opportunity and become best known. Please note the position has authority, constraints, guidelines, organisation structure etc. Which will be same from person to person, but some emerge over and above the role, they carve their name in history. Even if they leave, people recall their work, their contribution. Such type of people leave behind a legacy due to their work.

Now you will ask, how can one become best? The answer is keep improving keep innovating, enjoy your work, learn more and more about your work. Do that extra in your work, keep taking feedback, Implement the feedback to further improve, identify your customers, ensure you listen to customers, keep in touch with them and act on their feedback. When you try to show to the world that you are trying to become better and better in your role, you will be surprised that the world also brings to you such opportunities which will enable you to try new things and hone your skills more and more. Sad part is this is realised by very few as many always think such opportunities as "extra work" and / or "work for which one is not paid for." One must realise that payment comes after work and not 'first payment and then extra work.'

If you become best in your role at any moment of time, you become BRAND and then there is no stopping. You are in position to rule your future, people start identifying your name with the role and vice a versa. You become famous, you become role model of many. You become benchmark for many. You get immense fan following. It gives you immense fulfilment that your name is associated with the role / job or profession you are working in; Imagine how much this will give you remuneration benefit as well.

Many a times during interview of candidate, the candidate is asked a standard question: Where you see yourself after 5 years?" And normal reply is "I want to become manager" or "I want to lead this dept / function" No one replies that I want to be the best purchase professional, or I want to be the best R&D engineer etc. or I want to be the best team lead etc. Please note here, I am not talking anything different, What I am saying is if one is best project / purchase professional excelling in purchase processes and project management techniques, if one is best team lead, there are high chances that the person will be picked up to lead the purchase function as and when vacancy arises. To be manager or dept head is not in your hand but to be the best team lead, to be the best purchase professional is in your hand. Action is in doing your role better and better, becoming dept head is the result. be so good that when the organisation is looking for dept head / team lead role you become a strong contender for the same.

E.   *Be devoted to the role/job.*

Devotion to something means give it your full time, full attention, full energy. Be available to the organisation all the time. People even come to know if a person takes unnecessary leave or takes leave for non-legitimate reasons. Your availability also makes you a 'Go-to' person. This brings more opportunities to you obviously in form of work and gives you exposure. In case of a job what it means is not only 8 hours of your official work time but even before and after work time, keep thinking about your role, keep thinking about various issues that you face, keep thinking about solutions that you can try to resolve those issues / constraints etc. Please note you may have a commercial or technical problem but the answer you may get sitting in a restaurant or watching a TV serial or commercial. Do not take your job as something where you get paid for 8 hours presence so work should also be for 8 hours.

A graduate professional after joining an organisation very soon gets designations such as Asst manager and we all say that he /she is in a managerial role. Question here is one gets designated as manager, also becomes part of management staff, but does he /she thinks like a manager or still thinks like an employee. When you think like an employee you always keep management as if it (management) starts above you. But when you think like manager you believe that the buck stops at you. You think yourself as owner of your business (organisation's business). Your whole outlook changes, your approach changes, and it shows up in the way you act, you talk, you take decisions etc. These all things get noticed and you score high on sense of ownership.

This brings me to another way to look at your job.

When I meet any youngster who has started working, then normally they will tell me the name of the organisation where they work and along with name it is customary to also mention designation. Sooner or later a graduate gets designation of manager. I always ask them, are you an employee or manager? A general arrangement or shall I say conventional arrangement is of an employer and employee relationship. An employee thinking is "I have a job for which I get paid for and I just have to do what is expected from my job ." Employee type of people will refer to some entity as management while speaking about an issue or while speaking amongst colleagues or while chatting. It is like "Management starts above me" and "I am not management." But when you think that you are management, then your way of looking towards an issue or problem or work changes. Yes, at lower level of management you may have limited authority, but at least that much authority must be used as management. Management thinking is you think as if it is your own business.

Take a simple example of travel. Various organisations have travel allowances with pre decided limits depending on the cadre of the employee. Now one thought is you utilise what limit you have, and you are still right in your decision. Another thought is you spend judiciously and sometimes spend less than your eligibility. This way you demonstrate that you own the business and every spend you see as hit to company's profit.

Empathy is another way to demonstrate ownership. If you are in purchase, it is good to visit supplier's shopfloor, it is good to visit your shopfloor where your material is getting used in the next process. If you are in design function, it makes sense to sometimes visit your shopfloor, visit customer sites where your product is used, have connect with service personnel because they know what difficulty is faced at site. These things demonstrate your orientation towards not only external customer but also internal customers.

Your ability to manage risk and avoid potential damage to the organisation also indicates your devotion to the organisation. This shows that you are good in managing crisis. Generally, it is customary for a function to blame other function for any failure. Even if you may be right but in the process organisation suffers. Hence you should be in position to foresee potential problems and ensure actions are taken, even if it has to be taken by other functions, in order to ensure organisation as a whole does not suffer.

It is important to take total ownership and unless you give it your full, you will not be devoted, and this will affect your performance which will be visible to others. We have heard terms like love your job, being married to one's job. All this means same thing, being devoted to your job.

F. *Enjoy your job*

I remember during my visit to Japan almost 30 years ago, in one training programme the way sensei (Japanese word for teacher) explained their thought process, made amply clear to me why Japanese have excelled in zero mistake work. They have synthesised work as:

This almost matches with Maslow theory but has been explained in a very simplified manner.

When one is at worker level, the difference between work and sport is very clear, Work is to earn money, sport is to spend money. People work so that they get money in order to spend the same on enjoyable things like sport, games, entertainment etc. Here the aim is work as much which is needed to earn that much money. But as one moves up, one starts thinking about work as a source to create that enjoyment, one starts looking for enjoyment within work and not outside work. So, the difference between work and sport becomes obscure, work is no more to earn money, but work itself becomes enjoyment. Let us analyse when we enjoy and what we get out of enjoyment. We get pleasure and satisfaction when we experience joy. Satisfaction is also a kind of fulfilment. Now let us come back to work: If we take work as mere task then it is difficult to derive fulfilment or pleasure. The task may be small, but it might be an element of a big project. We all have heard the story of three mason, each of whom were doing the task of laying bricks.

When asked what are you doing?

First one said: I am laying bricks.

Second one said I am building wall.

Third one said I am building temple (the larger picture)

So, if you keep larger picture in mind, you will be deriving fulfilment, pleasure even from a small task being done by you. Knowing details about your job, knowing what is expected from the point of view of Quality, Delivery (timeline) and Productivity (efficiency) will give you more involvement into your task and you will scratch your brain to think how to better in all these three aspects of the task. The more you scratch your brain and get involved the more you will be devoted to your job. The more you are devoted to your job the more it will be visible that you are not just carrying out a task you are told to, but you are applying your mind in it. All this will make your execution better and better.

I once again reiterate that whatever role / job function you get chance to work in, do it with full devotion. If you are enjoying doing that role, this fact does not get hidden from others and it helps in you doing it better and better and hence your personality is manifested in ways as explained above. Just imagine if you are not enjoying the job, you will remain absent occasionally and then it gets noticed and you are labelled as not reliable. But if you are putting your mind, most of the time you will do well and even if you are not getting result, your effort will be visible.

G. *Be resourceful, Be a likeable person.*

Be a person whom, when people see, they feel happy, they have good memories not recall of bad events. Be a person whom people, even if they are from other functions, like to meet and interact with. Hone your interpersonal skills to have good relationship with your colleagues and seniors from other functions. This increases your ability to get help from other functions and makes you a valuable resource to your boss. Some people develop very good rapport with outside agencies / Govt bodies. Such people are important resource. Some people develop good rapport with some tough customers, such people are seen as crisis managers in the organisation.

Some people do very good networking, even with their counterparts in competing industry, they also become a good resource.

H. *Do not get into a group/coterie.*

In organisation groupism is a normal phenomenon. It is also natural for us as a person to like some people, see more comfort in being with certain group of individuals. Let that be, however, you must not get labelled as someone who belongs to a group. Efforts to be made in this direction in a conscious manner.

1. Never become informer about certain people or certain seniors.

2. Avoid sitting beyond your work requirement with any of the seniors in their cabin.

3. During breakout time, sometimes at least sit for coffee in a group which is not your normal group.

4. During meeting, in conference room, sit with people who do not belong to your dept or function.

5. There are occasions when dept picnics are arranged, join these events and also ensure you are not seen all time only with certain people.

When you are not seen as part of a group or favourite of someone, your acceptance is high. A high acceptance increases your chances of nomination in teams, it also helps you in getting favourable response from other functions, your own dept colleagues. Please note you will not be able to do your work, complete your assignment unless you are in position to get positive response from whom you are seeking the help or co-operation. You should not be labelled as someone's person, it does more harm than bring benefits in the long run.

I.   *Do not say 'NO' to management.*

Management in many cases is your boss, sometimes it can be also more senior level. When they advise you to take up certain special task, or work in a different city, or work in a different function, do not say 'NO.' As team member you must work to strengthen the hands of your boss. Please note that assignments come only to those who have potential to complete them. Never take it as punishment. Many a times your well-wishers may advise you otherwise but go with your boss's gut feel. If you find he wants only you to take up a particular assignment, accept it and see to it that you shine even in that role however low profile it is or low visibility the role may have, however difficult that task may be. Do it and do it well with full involvement.

Career

Career is a word used and spoken about many times, more frequently but less seriously. I can categorise people in their early years under the following categories:

1. Those who are very clear (at a very early stage in their life) what they will be doing in their life, and which career they will pursue.

2. Those who are not yet clear in their life about what they will be doing but (I repeat but) are very clear that whatever opportunity destiny puts in front of them, they will do it very well and embrace anything next that comes their way. These people many a times somewhere later in their journey figure out what will be the path / profession they will pursue in their life. But also many a times they do not and hence end up working, be the best, in whatever they find destiny bring their way.

3. Those who are always dissatisfied, who know more than what they can chew, who make their life very complex and, in the process, lead a complicated life. These are the people who are normally unhappy and dissatisfied with the opportunity they get, make mess of it, and always

think that the next opportunity that will come their way / or that they will seek will give them satisfaction and then only they will be happy. You will find many like these around you in your family, among your college friends, in your office.

So, the point is career relates to your education that you acquire, but it need not be the cause or reason to where you end up your career after the age of 60 years plus. Career is a very dynamic phenomena and changes its course based on decisions you make, choices you make in your life journey. Career planning is word used quite often, but I do not have cases where I can say a career was planned meticulously right in beginning and it worked. To me, career is not a linear curve and is filled with uncertainties. A very sedate career has been seen as suddenly taking a big lift just at the onset of an opportunity one gets. Let me put forward my observations:

A. Career is a marathon, a long-term phenomenon, it is not a T20 Match which gets over in limited time.

Career is not a T20 match, but it is like a test match. Like in a test match, where one builds innings session by session, change strategies session by session, paces innings well to build a good score at the end. In your career also you need to build it over time, change your approach as time passes, decide what worked and what did not work overtime, under different situations in order to end the career at a high, at a fulfilment level. There will be times in your working tenure when you will find things going your way, but you will also come across times when you will find things not going your way. What shall be your approach in both these situations? There will be times when you will be extremely unhappy with the appraisal process as you will not find the reward as per your expectation. There will be times when you will have to struggle with results in the role that you are in or in the project assignment that you are asked to lead. There will be times when you / yourself must be realising that you are not giving output as per the expectations of your team lead. There will be times when some personal issues and family issues will be disturbing your work output in office. There will be times when you are offered job enrichment, but you are asked to re-locate and your family responsibilities will be holding you back. There will be times when you and your boss are not at the same wavelength. If so then for some time, to gain trust do what boss wants you to do and how boss wants you to do. In cricket also it is said when the match starts, in the first hour of a test match, play with straight bat, it means do not take risks or get into any adventurous act.

Assess the pitch for bounce, turn etc so that you adjust your game and pace your game accordingly. Similarly, Career must be nurtured very cautiously. You need to build upon opportunities in your career as time passes,

The points that have been brought -up in the book so far will give you the way out. As I have said many a times in this book, I will repeat again WORK WORKs. You must first and foremost ensure that your work is not suffering. If you are putting efforts to balance your family issues, and ensuring that your work is not suffering, this will come to the notice of your team lead. Your dissatisfaction with the appraisal outcome, should be responded more in the form of work. In cricket there is phrase "Let your bat do the talking." It is used in situations when a player is dropped from national team or World Cup squad. It is then used to communicate that let that batsman show good score in other tournament matches and this is the only way to come back into national squad. However, if the batsman gets so much discouraged and starts scoring low in other matches, it in a way, justifies the drop from national team or world-cup squad. If on continuous basis you find that the organisation is not able to offer you higher elevation or job enlargement and you find that your learning in the current role has stagnated, you have choice to look for new organisation. However, even in your attempt to join a new organisation, please note the way you have conducted yourself so far, worked so far, will be the most influencing factor.

B. Be a good learner: You must take responsibility for your own development.

You have been a student in the first phase of your life. Continue being a student always, even after your studies are over. I wonder when Guru Purnima, (Teacher's Day), is celebrated every year, why Student's Day is not celebrated every year. This universe teaches you every moment, one has to have an eye for it. Throughout your daily sting in your organisation, you may come across a good presenter; learn a few tips from here; you may come across a good discussion in a meeting, observe and learn how points are made and argued, and may find a person who is always formally dressed, learn dressing from here. You yourself will realise who is good at what. There are things as simple as how to stand, how to sit, how to eat, how to think, and how to speak, which you can learn in your journey. You come across so many people, and if you are keen to learn, you will be able to spot good examples and successful examples that you can emulate. Reading good books and going for further education in the profession you are currently working on are the ways one keeps himself / herself updated. A sales professional can take courses on sales processes, customer management, etc. A person in production can take courses in productivity management techniques, industrial engineering, and labour laws, labour Management, Workplace upgrades, etc. In our times, we used to attend part-time courses, which involved travelling in the evening after office hours. Today, it is quite convenient; you have various courses being offered online, and you must have the inclination to learn, and apply what you have learned, in your work area.

Good organisations do have various management as well as technical development programmes. One gets nominated for it. Some organisations allow employees to choose programmes based on their role and cadre. People do attend but one who gets benefitted is the one who implements the learning in own's area of work.

So, being a student is a need.

Japanese propagate the following for someone or some organisation to be a good student:

People who want to learn must have a student-type mindset.

> Especially when so much information overload is around.

A student means to be a person with great skill,

Four things are needed in a person:

1. Talent to grasp what is being learned

2. Basic things must be done properly. Understand the theory, also do first-level practice by implementing

3. Efforts to be put in to learn things well.

Look for a playing field where one can try these learnings

This is crucial to be a student, and the four approaches required are.

a. open mind

b. baby-like heart to believe in what is being taught

c. adult-like approach to thinking about how the teaching can be implemented

d. self-reflection after trying to internalise and improve further

It is essential that we remain students,

There is no need to show off what you know; make the world see what you are capable of, by implementing.

C. Assess in a gradual manner what motivates you, what you do best, and what you enjoy doing.

As explained earlier, among the many jobs that you do in your workplace, there will be certain parts that you must be doing extremely well. Others see you as doing very well. It is a cyclic phenomenon as others will come to you to get help from you for such work. You must keep judging yourself and identify what those things are. Yes, it takes time, but over a period, it happens. This way, you will know what your sweet spot is. You also will not be saying no to such work. Slowly, you may think and take a call about whether that can be your next career switch.

To give you one example, Take a person working in a purchase function. Now, as per the standard job description in purchase, one must work in the areas of supplier management and material management. Interaction with suppliers and factories, controlling inventory, doing the right pricing, and material planning can be work elements, to name a few. But if people find you very apt in downloading information/ data from SAP. You know a few SAP commands where you can run queries to extract the required information. Many of your dept colleagues, your boss, must be turning to you whenever they are in need of such type of data from historical records. Here, you will slowly realise that you like working on the SAP Materials Management module and that you do a good job there. You then assess that SAP can be your next career move. We all know SAP implementation requires material function experts. So, this is one way, even if you are not clear in the early part of your journey, you can gradually get an idea about what area you enjoy doing and hence can be part of your career plan.

So, while you are in a role, another you within you must keep identifying what you enjoy and are good at. This is one way to get into a niche career over time.

I recall the pyramid diagram we used to define an organisation; we highlighted that as one goes up in the organisation, larger teams / bigger responsibilities come in. Many times, these require good managerial skills and less technical skills. As you get to the higher and higher ladder in an organisation, technical skills requirements reduce. But if your own assessment, as described in this section in the above paragraphs, convinces you that you like technical stuff and enjoy doing technical stuff, then there are no issues as people do choose to remain technical and not go for higher managerial levels. They do get salary hikes and may not get those kinds of designations like GM, CEO, etc. Some organisations have a system of defining such categories of employees as HSE (Hot Skilled Employees).

When we look around, there are examples in cricket where Sachin Tendulkar tried captaining the side; he realised that it was better for him if he relinquished this role and concentrated on his batting. Amitabh Bachchan tried himself in politics but soon realised that it was better for him to pursue full-time acting. Nothing wrong if one retracts from some venture which was not so successful.

D. *Keep an eye on what the organisation wants.*

While working in your current role, you must keep your eyes/ears open and sniff what is going on in the organisation.

Various meetings that you attend, in cross-functional and in seniors' presence, you can sniff this.

Examples can be:

1. Any change initiative

2. Any important long-running order execution

3. Any new expansion inside or outside the country

4. Any new product design initiative

5. Any IT initiative which cuts across various functions

It would be good to say "yes" if you were given the opportunity to be part of any such organisation-wide initiative. It helps you in the following way:

1. You get to learn something new. Upskill yourself.

2. Your CV gets improved as you learn something new within your function: updated CV with 'current' things in the market.

3. You get exposure to colleagues, cross-functional: Higher visibility.

4. You get exposure to your department seniors and other seniors: You are the one identified in your department for that initiative, so it is your job to update your bosses from time to time

You can see from the above it is a win-win situation not only for you but also for your organisation.

E. *Be the best rat, even if it is a rat race.*

Critics do call it a rat race, and even if it is so, try to be the best rat in the rat race. This takes you back to the earlier section, which says to be the best in whatever role you get. Many of the observations and behaviour patterns mentioned above help you to be the best. The point being driven here is, though rat race has a negative connotation if you are in the mud, you have to be the best till the time you are there. Work does not stop just by taking yourself out, saying it is a rat race. If you are in the race and are among rats, then you better put effort into being the best. It helps you as you are the best, so you have so much more chance to come out of it when the time comes.

F. *Work in a different culture; do not avoid it if opportunity forces you do this.*

To be a professional, you must have experience of working in different cultures. Different cultures can be as simple as different bosses in the same function. Different functions at the same location, at different locations but functions can be the same or different. Even different countries but same organisation and finally different organisations. This brings in you resilience; it brings in you ability to face issues which many times are culture-based. When you look back at your career after 30/35 years of journey in the industry, you will recall how you embraced challenges due to cultural change and emerged a better professional / individual. It's like in cricket: unless you have played against different countries and on different pitch locations, you will not be seen as an accomplished player. Do not take these as punishment; embrace them and take them as challenges. Learn from them and emerge as better person. In a way, what I am indicating to you here is do not take this as "not a comfort zone." Embrace it, and take it as if it is an opportunity for you to test yourself out of your comfort zone.

As one grows in the management cadre, one must be more apt in assessing situations, weighing different constraints or factors and making decisions. Many of these skills come from exposure. Any opportunity where you find this exposure, you must try yourself.

In some organisations, there is a system of identifying people who have shown signs of leadership qualities or those who are generally good in performance and need to be tested in different situations to assess their leadership qualities. These people are then deliberately put in different functions (you may call it transferred to different functions) to give them exposure and hence develop them. While this is done, the employee may be made aware of the reason why the transfer is effected or may not, as the organisation might decide to keep it confidential. In both cases, you must be open to such changes and give yourself a try. As said earlier, you must give it all that you can and see what the result is.

In some organisations, unless a person has worked in different functions, the chances of elevation to next grade diminishes or slows down.

In 2006, I was asked to change over to manufacturing. After 24 years, I was going to have workmen also with me. The workers in my organisation were unionised units. During my first 24 years, though, I was involved in functions like Quality, Inspection and six sigma; since a lot of my work involved visiting the shop floor, some projects also included workers. I was carrying an image of dreadfulness if asked to deal with the union. It was shown that dealing with unionised workmen is not everyone's cup of tea and requires some special skills.

The first day of my joining, I was taken to meet the president of union, who also happened to belong to the workshop which I was to head. We had an introductory chat and he assured me for positive support.

The product line I was responsible for was having issues which constrained the quantity increase and hence our production numbers were below market expectation. The gap between demand and supply was talk of discussion in every management review.

It was a challenge to me that not only technical issues were to be resolved but also many human (Workmen) related issues were to be sorted out to make the workmen, engineer unit cohesive. I started communicating with workmen wherever I used to get a chance. I used to talk in broken Marathi. I had studied Marathi in school as a third language but did not practice speaking as the necessity never arose. Here, I got a chance, so I also honed my speaking, and it enabled better acceptance while communicating with the union. I learned that truthfulness helps and that if one can inspire the team, even if it is workmen, no matter what the rules are, one gets a positive response and results.

Though I left manufacturing in 2010, later when I came back as business head with responsibilities involving production as well, it helped as I carried out same approach and dealt with union at their leadership level while negotiating their demands.

G. Show resilience to withstand failures.

You may change jobs and then realise that it was a wrong decision as you did not adjust to the new organisation. Try the next organisation; it is normally not advised that you return to the same organisation that you left a few weeks ago. Once you have decided to leave, stay with this decision and try another opportunity. A return to the same organisation can be say after 8 to 10 years, as then you are not seen as a failed decision, but you come back with greater responsibility and more abilities. You may also come back to a higher designation.

Your project assignment may get into trouble, show up, try different things, and seek help; when this world finds someone struggling, people do respond with help. As mentioned above in this book, your effort is a significant factor, especially when you hit some roadblock.

You may get a tough boss; you may get a boss with whom your wavelength does not match. Go through this, see what works, see how you can make it work, once you overcome these your joy will be high, and your confidence will enhance.

An example is Mr. Amitabh Bachchan who is also known as Shahenshah of Bollywood, he had ten unsuccessful films before his film Zanjeer became a hit!

Current ruling party started with two seats in Lok Sabha decades ago and are now in majority in Lok Sabha for the second successive term. We all have seen that famous picture which shows a mountain with a hole in it, the message it tries to convey is solution to a problem is thought it, not by avoiding it or circumventing it.

H. *Do not change job just for salary rise. Now a days the culture is "what is the package."*

The package syndrome: Be aware of it. Now a days the culture is to talk of package. As soon as one joins an organisation, the person starts telling everyone about package. Your classmates, your friends, even your relatives speak of package.

Please note in this book, at the beginning itself, I said that 40 year journey is a career. So, your start does not always indicate where you will end and whether you will have a successful career. How you end your career is what will tell your success.

Money, especially in the first half of a 40-year career, if not in full career, should be the byproduct. I am not saying that money is not important. I am saying that money should not be the vehicle of deciding factor to switch jobs. Money should be the outcome, the effect, the lagging indicator, the monitor of your career. Your effort shall be to change jobs if you find the new opportunity will bring in core skills in you, the new opportunity will give you larger responsibility like leading a team of employees, the new opportunity is giving you some new exposure which will make you a better and more skilled professional. Another reason to change jobs can be that you get to work in a structured/large company where there are more development opportunities. Another reason can be you get work in a role in which you have, by now, assessed that you do well, but your current organisation is unable to give you a chance in that role.

You should never disclose your package to anyone. In fact, these days, organisations do mention in the reward letter that if the package / CTC (Cost To Company) is disclosed, it will be taken as a breach of conduct. Not only within your organisation but even in your family, your package should not be known to anyone. The peer impact and the societal impact are so huge that you will get into a pressure game and will make the wrong decision. You must develop an ability to see yourself vis a vis others in your organisation and then take a call if you find it right to change jobs.

Mental toughness is key when one finds that peer pressure/societal pressure is high.

Give you one example from cricket: *If anyone is asked which name comes to mind if we think of a player who scored maximum centuries ever, then the name is Sachin Tendulkar. However, Sachin scored his first hundred in not his first, second or third match, but in his 78th match!! Hope you digested this information?*

He made his one-day debut in 1989, but it took five years for him to score his first one day hundred! He did it in 1994. But later there was no stopping and he holds record of most one day hundred! Very recently Virat Kohli surpassed his record in 2023.

Take another example: *Mr Mohammed Azharuddin holds a record of centuries in each of the first three test matches successively! However, people do not know him as a centurion record holder when he ended his career.* So, a good package at a start does not mean the end will be good after 40 years, a bad package at the start does not mean the same will be bad at the end of a career.

What you get at the start, where you work in your first job, has no connection with where you end your career. I am not saying that one should not start with a higher package or good company. What I am saying is if it has happened so, let it be. Where you end your career depends a lot on what you do in this journey called 'career.'

I.   *Have a mentor.*

We spoke of resilience against failures, we spoke about getting skilled, we spoke about relativity in this world, so handling mental pressure is very important. The way this world is moving, most of us will know how to be physically fit, as a lot of WhatsApp knowledge floats on exercise, food habits, etc. The way the number of gyms is flourishing also indicates the same. You will not be under financial pressure as you will be earning enough for your basic needs. What will be difficult to manage is mental pressure. So having a mentor is extremely useful in one's career.

The mentor can be your mother, father, brothers, friends, college teachers, family member, a senior colleague, even your boss! A mentor is one who you think, I repeat who you think, gives you advise without any self -interest. He or she need not be a well-qualified person but someone who knows you, who knows society and organisation dynamics will be able to give you lot many advice when you seek. When things do not go your way, or when you get conflicting inputs, it is the mentor whom you can turn to. If mentors happen to be from industry background and with versatile experience it is the best as they give lot of advise which will be enabler to you to do well in your organisation based on the role you are in.

I remember when I came to sales from manufacturing, my mentor advised me to travel a lot. To travel 15 to 18 days in the month. I implemented it and it expedited my initial phase settling into this change role.

J.   *Develop a hobby.*

Continuing from the above paragraph where I spoke about ability to handle mental pressure, it helps if you can develop a hobby. It can be in any area such as photography, travelling, singing, even acting, reading, sports etc. This helps to rejuvenate you from work pressure, and it also sometimes helps you to develop a network, which may be of benefit in your professional career. You can even have a work element as your hobby. For example, sales professionals may like meeting new people, spending more and more time at marketplace. An R&D professional may like indulging in some research projects through academics' support. These are the ways you can relax. If your hobby is related to your work, then you will have double benefit as your work will be much more enjoyable to you and obviously the output will be excellent.

K. *Grow vertically in the organisation.*

We see people hopping for jobs at regular intervals. It is said and being quoted is 'if one does not change job in 4 years, then it is believed that something is wrong with the person.' I find this absurd.

You should grow vertically in the organisation. What I mean here is at least 2 or 3 promotions must happen in the organisation. This will convince you that your value is seen by the organisation, it also gives you exposure of leading a team, where you also learn and develop man management skills, very essential for a professional. Remember in this book, we spoke about organisation structure being pyramid so when you grow means you go up the ladder. When this happens, it indicates that you have been chosen from a group of people for higher responsibility. it gives you confidence and also a belief that the way you are working is 'working.'

Changing job too frequently may fetch you a better package but you will always be vulnerable as you are yet to prove yourself. It is generally seen that in a span of 40 years two or three job changes are professionally beneficial. Here it means in an organisation you spend 10 to 12 years, before you switchover to another organisation. Job switching after good experience at one place helps you to learn different cultures, different industry, different market types, different product/processes. For example, a good sales professional would not like to limit himself/herself to say a Pharma industry, a stint in FMCG and Healthcare can broaden outlook, as sales professional, of an individual. A CEO of chemical business would like to gain more professional expertise, try his/her skills in another industry such as logistics, food industry. But these changes make sense only after you have grown in your present organisation and not only developed yourself but also have delivered towards the organisation success. It is relatively easier to rise by moving horizontally than by moving vertically, which when too frequently done does not help in career.

L.   *Learn to give time, time.*

It matches with (A) above. A career is never a linear progression. At any moment it can take a jump, but one never knows when.

Just to share with you my career progression, pl read the table below.

Time Period	Role	No of Reportees
1983-1998	Quality Assurance	Max 02
1999-2005	Quality & Six SIgma	0
2006-2009	Manufacturing	53 Engineers, 113 Workmen
2010-2014	Sales & Service	300 Engineers
2015-2020	Head of Business	1200 Engineers, over 900 Workmen, 1500 on-contract Workmen, 200 on-contract Engineers

I am asked how come I managed to work in roles of different nature. My answer is: I just kept working in the roles that were offered to me and time took its course. With time I learned, I matured, I developed myself into a better professional, human being with wider outlook, with better and better understanding of organisation working, with better interpersonal skills and above all getting macro view of an organisation.

What it means: Career is not linear progression and also the convention that one must have good number of reportees, is not always true, because now a days many organisations have matrix reporting where you might be reporting to more than one boss, or vice a versa where you as boss, will have team members who also will have another boss. (Sharing of resource) So your success depends on how you can influence and get work done. Please note as I have indicated in this book, to be successful in your assignment, you will need contributions from many people from more than one function, so your ability to extract support from them will be key. what is your contribution to the team, function and / or the organisation is important.

Career is never linear: *When I joined my organisation as Graduate Trainee. We had many in our group recruited from various colleges in India. Let me share with you my journey vis a vis two of my joining batchmates. I joined the Quality Assurance function. My batchmate Naj joined sales Function and another batchmate Rusheel joined Process Development function. Rusheel was an IITan, mentioned here because almost the first 20 years of our journey Rusheel was one year ahead of both of use whenever promotions happened. Since he used to get promotion one year earlier to us, we used to say, 'he is IITan!' and sort of console ourselves. A time came when his progress slowed down and Naj got ahead of us. By this time, we were quite mature and hence never sought any explanation for this. By the time we were into the journey of 32 years and it so happened that I got the final promotion one year ahead of Naj, and I was not only Immediate Superior (boss) to Rusheel but next Superior to Rusheel. We three continue to be friends. Our functions were such that it never had any direct comparison as we had different bosses always.*

M. Financial Planning

It is a vast subject, but I just want to make two suggestions here. It is generally seen that you start your career and start earning by the age of 22 plus minus 1 year. I recommend that right from your first salary you start saving. You may say money is fulfilling many needs and 10% reduction is not possible. The concept these days is not to save what is left, it is save first and spend what is left. At the beginning it does not matter if you get 10% less salary than what you have been offered. You assume that you get 10% less salary and you must inculcate the habit of saving on a monthly basis 10% of your salary. It can be through SIP in Mutual fund connected with large cap or flexi cap or index fund. However, if you are averse to the Shares Market, then you also have the choice of contributing an extra 10% to your PF account. As you know, the company deducts some percentage from your salary and adds their own contribution every month to your PF account. Here many organisations allow what is called VPF, where your contribution can be increased. So, the choice is yours, you add an extra 10% to your PF (debt type of investment) or you start an SIP in Equity based Mutual Fund. Please note over the long run say 10 years or more, Equity has given higher returns. This is one way you develop capital which can be of use at some point in your life.

By the time you reach 28 years of age, it is a good idea to buy a home. It need not be a home where you one day will stay. It must be a home where you can afford a house by taking a housing loan and good chance of appreciation in price over years. The idea here is you get the best interest rate as you can apply for loan tenure of max permissible years. Your age being 28 or less you will get a longest period loan and by the age of 48 to 50, you will come out of this loan. Income tax benefits (old scheme) you avail, once the house is ready it fetches you rent, so all in all your EMI almost gets covered up. As your salary increases over time, this EMI will be smaller percentage of your salary. Once you are 48 to 50, you have a choice then to buy a house where you will stay. At that time this current house (you had invested in) sale amount is a capital which you can use if need be. Please note here, the suggestion of buying house is not from the point of view of whether you need a house or not. It is irrespective of your family background. It is from purely financial management angle as you build a capital over time.

The second suggestion is to go for term insurance, I reiterate, simple term insurance for your life. The earlier in your age you take this the less will be the premium for a good amount of coverage throughout your life. There are many schemes which give other benefits along with life cover. Take the one which gives only life cover.

Illustration from few real-life examples:

An Example:

I joined my organisation in 1982 as trainee. Got placed in Quality dept, which was not my choice. Like many of us, I also wanted R&D. At that time one of my well-wishers who was head of R&D in another organisation and a family friend had advised me to leave this organisation, once he came to know that my placement is in Quality dept.

Though I had one more job offer letter in my hand, I decided to continue (I probably is of the type, do best in whatever come your way and leave rest to destiny). My journey for about 17 years went smoothly with a long stint in the Quality Department. In the mean while I got chance to qualify for a scholarship for training in AOTS Japan. The course was QCTC (Quality Control Training Course). This changed my thinking about statistics and its application in statistical quality control. I also got exposure to "how Japanese think Quality" while undergoing different professors' sessions and factory visits during my course in Japan. I was in Japan for this course for 44 days. I also did my Diploma in Operation

Management (DOM) through University of Mumbai. I also did my Diploma in SQC (Statistical Quality Control) at ISI (Indian Statistical Institute) a body affiliated to government of India. Things were going smooth and in 1994, My business group decided to go for ISO 9001 certification, this was led by my department head. Hence, I also got involved in this initiative helping him in various activities. In the process, got certified as Lead Assessor for ISO 9001. Hence all indicators were set, and I was a full-fledged Quality professional who could have headed Quality Department one day.

Things turned, in the year 2000, my group head got to know about six sigma as a methodology for breakthrough results which GE implemented in improving various business processes to derive business success. He got a book titled "The vision of six sigma: A road map for breakthrough." He gave this book to three people in our group to read and make a presentation to him. I was the only person who read it and made few slides and initiated a presentation meeting with him, in my meeting apart from a few seniors, including my department head (Boss) the two other colleagues were also present who were given this book. After I presented, my group head (Who also was Director and member of the board in our organisation) decided that we will go for this initiative, and I was given the task to lead this initiative throughout the group.

I started driving this initiative in the year 2000. Up to the year 2003, I did not have six sigma word in my designation. It still was Quality Assurance and Reliability. The reason I am not aware but might be that having designation named six sigma would have made me put all eggs in one basket. Six sigma would have been a time bound initiative. Quality Assurance Reliability is forever and age-old traditional function in any organisation. So careerwise I was safe with this designation. In 2004 I was asked to move to another department called strategic initiative and do "only Six sigma!!" Many of my well-wishers in the organisation, told me not to opt for full time six sigma, as they felt it was a timebound role, and may sideline me. It's like out of sight hence out of mind. I was in a dilemma. I liked the topic six sigma and since it was asked by top management, I decided to accept it and give it everything that I can.

Come 2005 end, six sigma by this time had matured in depth and width throughout the organisation. I was told to changeover to manufacturing. See how a person who was fully dressed up with qualifications, certifications exposure to Quality, did not become Quality head but is now into manufacturing, heading manufacturing of one major product line. Later in 2010, I was offered sales. In 2014, I took over as head of business.

Learnings:

I used to think I was going to becomes Quality professional and may go up to the role of Head of Quality Department. Though it was in my mind, it never was in my hand. But what was in my hand was doing more and more in the role that came my way as given by the organisation. I also accepted a role, with a limited future but needed by the organisation at that moment. This was when six sigma came my way. All the above gave me exposure and helped me show my capabilities, which brought me opportunities in manufacturing and then sales. Please note, had I continued in Quality, I would never have got the chance to get into sales. When it came to business head, probably amongst choices available to top management I was the only one who had wide exposure to Quality, manufacturing and sales so I became an obvious candidate. I did have to surpass a few senior colleagues for the role of business head but maybe my wide acceptability as a person scored there. This might have given management confidence that I would be able to carry everyone along. Let me mention here that none of the changes mentioned in this paragraph about role or function were asked by me. It came to me, and I kept working. So, WORK WORKs.

Another example is:

In late 90s our business group decided to go for SAP implementation covering all functions. It was extremely prestigious project, which was to encompass all processes, functions including sales offices. It was going to be long-term project of more than a year of work involving team members who were to almost work full time along with SAP USA. A big team was formed with representatives from various functions. My department (Quality) was represented by Mr. Kratakar who was my immediate superior. I had a colleague named Mr. Droop who was my junior.

As time passed and the initiative got into implementation phase, a lot of activities needed to be carried out on PC (Personal Computer), using SAP software. Kratakar, though was the official team member and aware of processes involved in Quality, was not able to devote full time due to other responsibilities. Droop was good, interested and proficient on PC as well as quick to understand software. Kratakar knew that Droop likes getting involved in SAP related activities and since he (Kratakar) had other responsibilities, he found Droop a helping hand for doing various tasks which were asked by the SAP team to carry out in Quality function towards implementation of SAP.

As the assignments from the team on SAP project increased, Mr. Kratakar started involving Droop and seeking his help more and more. Droop, liking the work, started taking more and more interest in the assignments in SAP to be carried out and expected from Kratakar, representing Quality Department. Slowly the tasks increased and hence the involvement of Droop.

Understand the situation here, Mr. Kratakar is an official nomination, but Droop got into doing more and more work which used to come his way through Mr. Kratakar. Other team members in the SAP team from different functions came to know about this in a gradual manner and understood that Droop does most of the work on SAP to help Mr. Kratakar complete the other task needed from Quality function. Naturally, they started going to Droop directly. Droop was responding so well that sometime even at 5:39 pm (Our shift closing was 5.40) if he used to get a call seeking help, he would restart the PC, complete the activity what is being requested and then only leave. The more Droop responded, the more work came to him, the more he became known to the SAP team and others that he is very good in SAP. By solving various issues Droop got enough enhancement of skills which made him a trained SAP professional who, pl remember, was not an official nominee in SAP team.

The whole project was successfully implemented. Later my organisation's Infotech vertical decided to take SAP as a business vertical. This happened as it was found that while working with SAP service providers our team had gathered enough expertise in implementation of SAP in an organisation of size and complexity as big as ours.

The Infotech vertical wanted functional experts from various functional areas, including Quality. It would have been obvious for the members who were in the original implementation team to be asked to move to the Infotech vertical. Mr. Kratakar was not keen to move to Infotech vertical's SAP business and hence one can guess who became the obvious choice?!

It was Droop who got a chance, moved to SAP IT and even today is at senior position in our Infotech company. The organisation was happy that they got the right skilled person, Droop was happy that he got assignment for doing work which he enjoyed.

Learning from the above example is even if Droop was not an official member, he did not take himself out but respected that his senior is picked up for the team, however kept working on opportunities that came to him. At the beginning these were given to him by Mr. Kratakar and looking at the way he responded, took interest, other function people directly started coming to him seeking help. He responded and executed so well that the organisation started to know him. Please note while Droop did these SAP related assignments, his normal work was not allowed to suffer. What I mean here is that for this period SAP work was an additional work for Droop.

When the organisation needed SAP Quality Module professional as functional expert in newly created SAP vertical, he was the man. So, WORK WORKs.

Another example is:

Devdut was a B Commerce graduate when he joined our organisation. Since no vacancy was there and B Com graduates were not getting direct on-roll job as per company policy, he was taken on third party contract. This means he was on roll of an organisation who used to supply manpower for certain type of job such as those which were of a temporary nature and short time bound. Imagine the day Devdut would have got this job, anyone would have advised him not to take it as it was temporary nature of job with no possibility or very low possibility of a regular lifetime employment.

However, Devdut took it positively, because even though it was a temporary nature job, it was in a good organisation. He thought that he will get good exposure which will help him develop skills preparing him for the next fulltime on roll job. Please note here there was no history of person joining as third party roll getting on roll later.

Devdut joined as off roll in 2008 and started working in service management cell with most of the activity being handled by him as back-office support.

Meanwhile he continued to upgrade his qualification and completed his PGD (Post Graduate Diploma) from a reputed management institute in Mumbai. Since he did his PGD in the supply chain he was given chance to work in supply chain (logistics) department. From 2011 to 2014 he worked in warehouse management, demand planning and because of his earlier service management background he also handled complaints of one of the newly introduced products of our organisation. Please note he is still off roll, but got additional qualification while working and became more skilled to get into better role (from back-office support to logistics) and also did not mind added role of customer complaint handling of one new product.

In the above period from 2008 to 2014 his contract was renewed two times, but he continued to be on third part roll.

During this period, Devdut got exposure in many functions, also acquired additional qualification and got chance to work in different teams and under different bosses. Here since his work was good, his attitude towards work was good, more than one bosses (evaluators) assessed him as valuable for the organisation.

In 2015 he was taken on full time roll after he was assessed through a selection process comprising of written test and personal interview.

Devdut continues to do well having got three promotions since 2015 and is getting rated as top performer each year.

Devdut showed a good attitude with many behaviour patterns mentioned earlier, acquired skills and above all waited for time to give his career the much-needed jump. Devdut is now on the right track.

Another example is:

Dalma is an Arts Graduate and an MBA in HR. She joined our organisation in 1984. During the initial phase of her career, she was into a role of secretary to one of the Regional Sales Heads. While in this role, she got involved in arranging the Regional Channel Partners conferences (a Sales function role) for the Channel Partners of her region.

She did the job so well that she was asked by senior management to also co-ordinate annual all India Channel Partners conference which used to be held outside India.

In 1999, when our group implemented SAP involving sales and marketing functions covering the channel partners across the country, she was an active member and, in the process, acquired proficiency in Sales and Marketing module of SAP.

2002 onwards our business decided to nominate HR partners, business unit wise. Dalma's qualification in HR and her interest and people-oriented nature brought her the additional responsibility of BU-HR for sales, marketing, and logistics team members. She was also a member of corporate HR team formed for the "Campus to Corporate" induction training of Graduate Engineer Trainees.

In 2006 she was in the core team for establishing Customer Interaction Centre (CIC). The team ideated and implemented successfully the process for CIC.

A time came when she was into the roles of:

- Support to the office of Sales Head covering two regions.

- Management of annual channel partners conferences outside and within country.

- Training and development of channel partners in the country

- BU-HR role in recruitment of off-roll engineers

- BU-HR role of managing annual appraisal assessment of sales, marketing and logistics staff.

- SAP data support.

By 2016 she rose to head the Channel Management function of North, South and East region and superannuated while in the position of DGM in our organisation. This level is maximum level which, so far, any female employee has attained in our group.

Learning from the above is, Dalma got a start in a traditional role but kept excelling in other activities as opportunities came her way. In addition to many of the behaviour patterns mentioned in this book it involved embracing opportunities of varied types also putting extra effort to excel in each of them which paid rich dividend in her career in terms of senior level position professionally and remembered for her role by 100s of channel partners across the country.

Joined as secretary and reached level of heading channel management!

You may note the start of career and where it ended!

Practicing something and then making it a habit over time for getting effective results.

Now let me touch upon the implementation side of what I have been talking about so far in this book.

It is highly likely that you will start implementing the above behaviour patterns in your working. However, I would like to reiterate once again that the behaviour must be seen repeatedly in you before you are branded accordingly. And hence there are four aspects you must keep in mind:

1.   Thoroughness

2.   Consistency

3.   Continuity

4.   Effectiveness.

What the above means is that for any act to give you effective results (Effectiveness) the first three must be in place.

To explain further, let us say that you discover that your energy level is not the same throughout the day and you get tired easily.

To enhance your health is your aim:

But this is only a desire or a monitor where you want to see change.

Action does not lie here. This is the effect that you want to see. This is the result that you want to see. The action lies somewhere else. The cause lies somewhere else.

Once you have decided to improve health and sustain energy level throughout the day, you will make a plan of action.

These actions are the items that you believe, if implemented, will give you the desired result (effect).

In this case the plan of actions can be:

P1: I will drink one glass of milk with some energy booster every day.

P2: I will do yoga every day.

P3: I will make a habit of getting up every day at 5:30 am

P4: I will go for bike ride every Saturday and Sunday

Please note that the plan of action must be auditable, like done or not done.

Let us take from the above, P2 for further elaboration.

Thoroughness:

This means whatever yoga exercises you have learned, you will do them thoroughly as per the teachings you have got.

Consistency:

This means that you will do yoga every day and not that when you find convenient, not do in case you are late from office the earlier day, not do when you are on tour etc.

Continuity:

This means you will keep upgrading your yoga as time passes. Means the exercises that you were doing in initial phase, will be enhanced as you add few more exercises, you may do some difficult exercises as days pass.

Effectiveness:

This is where you observe or monitor after a period if you find changes in your health, your energy levels.

Now the above is with the belief that once an action is decided, it will give you effective result if and only if the action is implemented thoroughly, done consistently and improved upon in continuation.

In case results are not found, like in this case you find you did not improve your health, then first audit check must be:

P2: was it done thoroughly.

Was it done consistently or occasionally?

Was any improvisation done?

If the answer to the above is not Yes, then better work on it before you conclude that action decided was wrong.

Now we use the above learning to our behaviour pattern which you have decided to practice.

You want to work on and improve your response:

You want to be seen as a person who is responsive. You cannot just say, okay I have decided that from tomorrow onwards I will be more responsive. You have to have a plan of action.

What can be plan of action?

P1: You will reply to your emails within 48 hours.

P2: You will clear all mail in your inbox within a week.

P3: You will use "delay delivery" facility in your email for putting reminders to yourself.

P4: You will call back all calls you missed in the day, after 6PM same day at least by giving one full ring to that same number.

P5: While going to bed, you will recall back what all promises, commitment you still have pending to be responded.

When you review, you will observe that all Ps, above, are to be acted upon by you and can be easily auditable as being done or not, being done consistently or not, being improvised upon or not etc. If answer is No, then you must go back and work on that aspect of action. This is called acting on the gap or difference.

This is also known as PDCA in Japanese management teachings. It says that anything personal or professional objective that you wish to do / achieve, you must have a plan of actions (P) that you will take. Then you must start doing (D) those plans. Instead of reviewing your wish or objective you must first check (C) and review if plan of actions has been implemented or not. If they have been implemented and still objective is not met, then you need to make fresh plans or intensify them if you find you are in the right direction but need to do more to meet your objectives. But in case you have not implemented the plan of actions then first act (A) on it

Summary

In this book I have attempted to share with you my experience on how youngsters who are out of college after completing their studies are unaware of certain behaviour patterns which damages or let me say negatively affects their career journey. As you found out in this book many behaviour patterns, almost all are in the hands of the individual and one must be aware of it. Rather aware of it much early (or at start) of career.

I have stressed a lot on importance of work. It is not only actual work but also the way you work, the attitude you show in work. People mention about luck and destiny as factors for going up the ladder in an organisation. My view is the vacancy opening, the position getting created may not be in your hand, but once it is open, then you being there and being picked as suitable for it is in your hand. The above points are ones which make you a fit candidate for that 'open' position. The opportunities that come your way depend a lot on your work and the way you work. Once you see opportunities you need to take that calculated chance (I will not call it a risk) and test yourself. The next assignment you will take, the next person you will meet, the next organisation you may join, who knows can prove to be a game changer in your career.

It's simple, you must be valuable. You must remain valuable throughout your career. You must be of value to your family, friends, colleagues, organisation and society. This is the only way this world recognises you, felicitates you, gives you importance and you derive not only monetary gains but also professional stature as you move on in your career. Look at sports, look at industry. Look at entertainment, it is full of individuals who start almost alike at the same level, do almost similar things but finally very few reach a level which many dream about. They become so valuable that they almost call the shot. These are the people who work on themselves, hone their skills, grab opportunities that come their way to demonstrate what they are and what they can do.

As simple as an example of family. Don't you think even in family being valuable matters. Amongst the family members, amongst brothers and sisters, isn't it that the one who is valuable, able to help / contribute, resourceful gets more importance?

The more valuable you can be to others, the more you get in return or paid for.

Take an example of steel:

Raw Steel

Toyota Car

Razor Blade

Rolex Watch

Do all get paid the same price per tonne? (below are indicative numbers just to drive the message) All have steel material in it as basic material.

Steel is 700 USD per tonne.

Toyota car will be 20000 USD per tonne.

Razor blade will be 0.8mn USD per tonne.

Rolex watch will be 15mn USD per tonne.

See how value addition changes the price, base metal is steel in all the cases.

In India we have a quote: "Khudi ko kar buland itna, ki khuda bande se khud puche, bataa teri raja kya hai." You should be so good that , God will first ask your wish before deciding.

A good employee is seen as:

1. You always do Quality work; excellence is always your hallmark with rare errors.

2. You are quick and give quantum of work. You are fast in your response, and your output is high.

3. You have an image of being very co-operative and a good team player.

4. Your work output exhibits that you have made use of your knowledge and experience.

5. You know the subject well, are an expert in your job.

6. You are disciplined and would be so even if there would be no check on you.

7. You are keen to learn new and undertake new responsibilities and are comfortable in adapting to changed conditions very quickly. In case of constraints, you try and apply your own mind to solve them.

8. You can be trusted with a job with utter confidence that it will be done the way it shall be, without any worry. Your image is once a job is given to you, it will happen.

9. You rarely leave a task incomplete and take it behind schedule.

10. You do the task almost independently and in case of difficulty find a way to overcome the same. You do not require too often hand holding.

11. You are clear, precise and to the point in expressing your views.

12. You have a habit of planning well which also involves good use of resources and organising various activities very well to achieve the objective.

13. You also try to foresee, look ahead to manage risks, optimise resources.

14. You try to do something more over and above defined task.

15. In your work habit, stretch is visible as called for, in the task.

16. You normally use latest, advanced technologies as an enabler to bring out quality and quantity output.

17. Your customer orientation to internal and external customers is part of your nature and work ethic.

You have the potential. People use the phrase, "I will do my best" which in my opinion shall be I will try and put more and more effort. Life, the career must be evolved over time, one never knows what the end will be and where will be the end finally. So, the above points will help you be there, be active there, be always there and be seen. It also will not only tell the world about you but more importantly tell you, about you. The next person you meet, the next job assignment you may get. The next team you may work with, the next training that you take may prove to be a game changer in your career and life. So never lose expectancy, keep doing it after all this world belongs to doers.

Once you get an opportunity it is up to you, what you make out of it. And this is applicable to all types of work be it in industry, sports, politics for that matter in any aspects of life.

As I said at the start of this book, these are my observations based on live experiences, which I used to analyse and learn from. If you are convinced, try to put it into practice, it will help you to do better in your career and life. Working hard, even at the cost of some enjoyment helps you enjoy and relax later in your life. Else you start enjoying it and take it easy in the early days of your career which makes you struggle throughout your life including post-retirement life.

Let us look at tree. We all notice that a tree one day flowers and then offers fruits to us. Isn't it good and makes us happy? But how many of us realise that the extent to which a tree grows above the earth surface, almost same extent it grows below the earth. The growth underneath is relatively more difficult, as it (root) must grow against resistance (earth). The stage of flowering comes later in life. The growth below earth is that struggle days. Which is not visible but extremely important and crucial for the tree to flower / fruit one day.

It is said, "it is difficult to get an opportunity to work in an organisation, but it is more difficult to rise and reach senior management level in an organisation and even more difficult to remain at top." Many teams won the World Cup but may be once or twice, but Australia has won the cricket World Cup six times out of 13 tournaments. So, Australians are branded as champions. This also can be said to be the difference between class and form. Your class shall be such that your career has a stamp of it. One must continuously work and prepare himself / herself for it so that suitability, capability is never a question.

As I close this book, I refer to what Rahul Dravid said on the occasion of 100th test match of R Ashwin. And I quote: Greatness is consistency over time, it comes from practice, it comes from constantly making changes, it comes from sacrifice, it comes from stubbornness, it comes from constantly evolving, growing, and learning. It comes from giving everything to a team that you have and everything you have to the craft. And doing all these things faithfully."

The call is yours, Good Luck!

I can be reached at tgirish904@gmail.com

thank you Rajani

Book: Straight from the Gut by Jack Welch

Website: https://youtu.be/ lwJkP4AyqvI?si=WlEczQmunGqwJQ4p a video tum chalo, hindustan chale

Website: https://www.youtube.com/ watch?v=TBdgZAbCDAg a video on "Girish Karnad as monk"

Rahul Dravid speech a video https://www.youtube.com/watch?v=RoAHjCtZr18

Book: Count your chickens before they hatch: By Arindam Chaudhuri

Teachings of Dr Hiroshi Kubota San, Japan

Harsha Bhogle at IIM https://www.youtube.com/watch?v=kaw_bKOkULM